BANFF
CANADA'S FIRST NATIONAL PARK

A History and a Memory
of
Rocky Mountains Park

by
ELEANOR G. LUXTON

Summerthought

Banff, Alberta

Banff: Canada's First National Park

Published by

Summerthought

Summerthought Publishing
PO Box 2309
Banff, AB T1L 1C1
Canada
www.summerthought.com

Printing History
1st edition – 1974
2nd edition – 2008

Library and Archives Canada Cataloguing in Publication

Luxton, Eleanor G. (Eleanor Georgina), 1908-1995
    Banff : Canada's first national park / Eleanor G. Luxton.

Includes bibliographical references and index.
ISBN 978-0-9782375-4-7

1. Banff National Park (Alta.)–History. 2. Banff (Alta.)–History. I. Title.

FC3664.B3L89 2008   971.23'32   C2007-906892-8

Front cover photo: Banff Ave., Banff. © Glenbow Museum, na-2977-37
Layout: Linda Petras
Printed in Canada by Friesens

TABLE OF CONTENTS

Foreword

This book, *Banff: Canada's First National Park,* was first published in 1974. Although many books covering the fascinating multi-faceted life of Banff have since been published, this book stands alone as a comprehensive history of Banff. It presents a layman's view of the geological development of the Bow Valley; traces the history of First Nations activity in the area; outlines the effect of the railway and the tourism it promoted; details the establishment of the national park; and highlights the accomplishments of the colourful and adventurous pioneers who settled here. Readers will find of particular interest the author's portrayal of the unique problems of a town within the borders of a national park, and the constant challenges that has presented.

The author, Eleanor G. Luxton, was inspired to write the book as a result of her family's deep connections with the early history of Banff and the Bow Valley. Arriving in 1862, Eleanor's grandfather, David N. McDougall, was a member of one of the earliest pioneer families in Alberta. Her parents, Norman and Georgina McDougall Luxton, were among Banff's best known early residents. Eleanor herself was a highly accomplished woman, having degrees in Education and History. She was a gifted teacher and a strong role model for her students. As an historian, she wrote and lectured on the history of Western Canada. Her book, *Luxton's Pacific Crossing,* based on her father's diaries of an incredible voyage across the Pacific Ocean in a modified dugout canoe, was first published in 1971, and then reprinted in 2002. During the Second World War, Eleanor studied mechanical drafting and worked on locomotive design for the Canadian Pacific Railway in Montreal. She was also an astute businesswoman.

Before her passing in 1995, Eleanor established the Eleanor Luxton Historical Foundation, with a mandate to preserve the history of Banff and the Bow Valley. The foundation continues to actively follow her wishes. It also supports scholarships in Western Canadian history at the

Eleanor Luxton, 1908-1995.

University of Alberta and the University of Calgary. Additionally, it provides grants to non-profit conservation and environmental organizations, and operates the Luxton family home as a museum, as well as carrying out other initiatives that contribute to her goal of keeping the rich history of the area alive.

The archival materials Eleanor assembled in her lifetime provide a colourful and previously inaccessible record of many aspects of the settlement of Alberta, especially the Banff and Bow Valley area. They are available to researchers at the Whyte Museum of the Canadian Rockies, under contract with the Eleanor Luxton Historical Foundation.

Ralphine Locke, Banff, 2008

Preface

In this book, I have endeavoured to explain how Rocky Mountains Park, the first National Park in Canada, came into existence, how it developed, had its boundaries changed many times to try to fill the needs of various periods of time and was ultimately divided into Banff, Yoho and Glacier National Parks. The geological emergence of the area from the dark mists of time and the development of life seem fascinating to me. So, too, are the early explorers, who searched for passes, but missed likely ones into this hidden valley and therefore from it to the west. Likewise the Indians, who penetrated it and explored its secrets, captured my imagination. I have tried to explain these things as they are related to the Park, not as the geologist or the historian or the naturalist might, but in non-scientific language so I might arouse my reader's imagination and bring to life the romance and history that lie here.

As the Park developed so did Banff, the town which came into being because of the Hot Springs. Being in an accessible and fairly central location in the Park, its growth was inevitable. This is not a complete history of Banff – only the story of its growth, in relation to the Park development, as a playground for the Canadian people. I have tried to share what life in Banff was and is. The problems of the Park and of Banff are one and the same. Likewise, the federal government, the Canadian Pacific Railway and the people of Banff have always been interdependent. Banff is known throughout the world; without the Park it would have had less significance. On the other hand, Banff offers amenities for the visitors to the Park, and; indeed, plays host for the federal government.

It is, of course, in a book of this size, manifestly impossible to mention the names of all the people who contributed to the development of Banff and the Park. I have not endeavoured to do so. Those whom I have mentioned in this story, have been chosen, because they seemed to me to be the people who, in their deep-rooted love for Banff and the Park, contributed most to building the resort which has given pleasure to countless visitors. To those other people of Banff, whom I might well have included, but was compelled to omit for lack of space, I ask both forgiveness and indulgence.

This book is an attempt to give the average reader a glimpse of the development of one of the beauty spots of the world and of the immense struggle of the federal government and the people of Banff to save that beauty. I have endeavoured to make the reader aware of the grandeur of nature, and, also, aware of man's duty not only to enjoy it but to preserve it.

It is very true that every author, who aspires to writing a book, has to rely on the assistance of many people for facts and encouragement. I wish to express my deep appreciation, for encouragement and assistance, to Dr. Lewis H. Thomas, Department of History, University of Alberta. Dr. George F.G. Stanley, Director of Canadian studies, Mount Allison University, read the manuscript and his suggestions and comments were much appreciated. Mr. Edward Hart of the Archives of the Canadian Rockies was most helpful and patient in finding source material for me. Mrs. Sue Baptie at the Glenbow-Alberta Institute Archives of Calgary was both cooperative and quick to send me needed references. Mr. W. Fergus Lothian, Historian, National and Historic Parks Branch, Ottawa, and Mr. John Bovey, Provincial Archivist of Manitoba were both kind and helpful. Superintendent T.R. Heggie of Banff National Park and his staff supplied maps and information. Warden Ed Carlton gave me time and information. Mrs. Lillian Wonders of Edmonton has my thanks and admiration for so ably adapting my ideas and requirements to the map. Finally, to the people who have been willing to talk to me of earlier days, I say thank you.

Banff, Alberta   Eleanor G. Luxton
1974

nature unspoiled by man

The Sound
of Silence

The valley, surrounded by magnificent yet mysterious peaks, was very quiet. Lazily, the river meandered along and the lakes reflected the vivid blue of the sky, the towering mountains, the evergreens and aspens on the shore. Spring was everywhere, in the snow patches, the delicate green of new leaf, the first purple sheen of the pasque flower.

A squirrel ran down a tree trunk to where a robin perched on a nearby bush. A mountain sheep looked over the river below, where a deer was having a quiet morning drink. In the long grass, at the edge of the lake, a moose gazed at its reflection.

Then there came a change.

A coyote gave a warning cry, a little breeze set the leaves to dancing, the muffled roar of the falls sounded louder, the animals faded away into the forest – as an Indian stole into sight. He, too, seemed to be listening and watching – but all he heard was the sharp crack as a beaver tail struck the water. An eagle circled very high in the sky.

I

The First
of All Things

Nature is the constant reality for those who live in the mountains. The mountains with their many moods draw our eyes to their majesty; the forests show us life being renewed even after devastating fires. Most of us have laughed at the antics of wild animals. We have been made happy or sad at some of the things nature has done to us, but we would not give up any part of it.

Visitors have always been aware of the beauty, the peace and the pleasure of the mountains. They have written books about camping or climbing expeditions and in every book one finds pages devoted to all nature's gifts. The sports' lovers are frequent visitors because the air is invigorating and free of pollution. The ill come to regain health. Countless thousands of people, even those who were here for only a day or two, come back, time and again, to enjoy nature, and the peace and awareness it brings to them. They take nature walks of one-half to two and a half miles either by themselves or in the company of a park naturalist.

1
THE PERIODS OF TIME

The valley of the Bow with its present life resulted from a growth of 550 million years, a fraction of the three billion years it took to form the continent in which it lies. In the earliest periods of geological time the valley of the Bow was not even formed, the mountains, that were to rise, were beneath a great waste of water in an inland sea. Yet there was movement, as forces within the earth thrust up and sidewise parts of the earth's crust in great blocks and slabs that rose high into the air, broke along faults (breaks in rock layers where one side has been displaced relative to the other side) and because of the great pressure often slid over one another. The inland sea retreated but lakes and shores were left. Erosion and deposition in the inland sea were constant.

Running water was steadily breaking down the rock, carrying sediment to the seabed. For 85 million or so years the sea advanced and retreated, breaking down the sediments but opposed by the building of the mighty interior thrusts.

In Banff National Park the rocks are from only the latest Precambrian period. These were thrust up from the mud laid down as sediment in the inland sea, hardened by pressure of weight into shales or argelites. Their purplish, greenish or reddish grey may be seen on the gentle slopes covered by tree or talus on Storm Mountain. Of life in the Precambrian only the youngest fossil algae are found.

The Palaeozoic Era from 550-220 million years ago was a time of ancient life forms and of rocks that are predominant in the mountains of the Park. Cambrian rock can be seen in the main ranges from Castle (Eisenhower) Mountain west of the Continental Divide. Lower Cambrian are the purple and pink quartzite (hard sandstone) and the purple and green shades seen on the tree covered slopes on both sides of the Bow river valley where there are pebble beds. Middle Cambrian shales, limestones (calcium carbonate) and dolomites (calcium magnesium carbonate) overlie lower Cambrian. These rocks are relatively hard and form steep cliffs and peaks seen from Castle Mountain to Lake Louise. Mount Stephen in Yoho National Park, with its shales, bears many of the fossils of Trilobites in the shale of this period. The Upper Cambrian, with its bright orange-brown shale, is seen in Sundance and Sawback Ranges.

Lower Ordovician, rock of grey limestone or shale, is found in the Sawback Range, Mount Murchison and Mount Sarbach on the Banff-Jasper Highway north of Bow Pass, and has Trilobites, Brachiopods (clams) and Mollusks. Mount Wilson has a top cliff of the Upper Ordovician-Mount Wilson quartzite, and Mount Murchison has a band of it.

The Devonian and overlying Mississippian rocks form the bulk of the mountains of the Front Range to Castle Mountain. Rundle Mountain shows clearly on its north face the Devonian-Mississippian sandwich, with the Rundle Formation of grey limestone on top, the brownish shale of the Banff Formation in the middle and the Palliser grey limestone on the bottom. Both Rundle limestone and Banff shale are composed of shells and fragments laid down in the inland sea millions of years ago. Below all that is the slope of dolomite of the Fairholme. These rocks show reefs, shell debris and limy mud in which are coral and stromatoporoids (cell-like structure, now extinct). The skeletons have been washed out leaving holes, and it is this same formation that is found in many of the oil fields of Alberta, in the reservoirs of Leduc, Sturgeon lake and other oil fields.

The Mississippian (Rundle Formation) does not yield easily to erosion and one sees its cliffs on the top of Cascade as well as Rundle. Stems of sea lilies (crinoids) and corals may be found in this limestone near the gondola lift on Sulphur Mountain, and these rocks, too, are of oil reservoir formation as in Turner Valley and Jumping Pound oil fields.

Pennsylvanian and Permian, known as the Rocky Mountain Formation, has dolomites, sandy dolomites and cemented sandstones distinguished by pinkish-grey or orange colour and containing few fossils.

The Triassic rock of the Mesozoic (Spray Formation) is dark coloured siltstone and shale, which breaks easily into smooth plates. For this reason it has been used in many Banff buildings, such as the Administration Building. An easy place to see it is at Bow Falls where the north bank is Mesozoic Triassic rock, while the south bank is Paleozoic Mississippian. Jurassic rock is found only in the Cascade and Bow river valleys. These dark grey and black shales which weather to dark brown are seen just southeast of Tunnel Mountain or in the old Cascade river valley below Lake Minnewanka. During the Triassic and Jurassic periods ammonites (coiled sea animals) and the large reptiles were common. The rocks of the Lower Cretaceous are the youngest in Banff National Park and are the dark grey shales and sandstones with coal seams, found near the entrance of the Park and on Cascade Mountain at Bankhead.

The rocks just described were formed over millions of years but were not yet the mountains as we know them. The inland sea was still over the land and not until the late Cretaceous period did the Rocky Mountains begin to rise. During the time of the reptiles the climate was mild, there were great swamps with ferns forty feet high, club moss one hundred feet long with trunks of four to five feet in diameter. Here the great reptiles roamed and fed on the edge of the sea.

The Rockies continued to rise and the seas to retreat through the Tertiary Period, the earlier part of the Cenozoic Era which extends from seventy million years ago to the present. The Rocky Mountains as we know them were finally forced up from the sediments of the sea bottom; mammals and modern plants came into being.

Over these millions of years of the late Mesozoic and early Cenozoic eras a great interior thrust forced up the layers of sedimentary rock under the sea to great heights in anticlines (arches or domes) and synclines (troughs). This intense upthrust from the west caused breaks or faults and frequently a block from the west would be forced over another block. So great was this thrust many folds and fractures resulted along faults, hence the strata may be parallel, vertical, horizontal, folded and even whorled upside down. The Front Range of the Rockies clearly shows these thrust blocks of younger and upper Devonian and Mesozoic in the higher parts. Of these the upper Cretaceous are coal bearing.

The coal was formed by the intense pressure of overlying sediments and rock for millions of years on the swamps where the dinosaurs had fed. Because of the thrust to the east and the subsequent erosion over a long period, the

Mount Rundle reflected in Vermilion Lakes.

anthracite coal is mined from Cretaceous rock on valley level, while on both sides rise Devonian limestones in the Rundle and Banff formations. Thus we have mountains of old rock over valleys of young rock.

The Front Range extends west to Castle Mountain where the Castle Mountain Thrust fault runs north by west from Simpson Pass on the Continental Divide across Copper Mountain up Johnston Creek, up the Pipestone Valley, and down the Siffleur River to and beyond the North Saskatchewan River. On the west of the fault the folding is synclinal (the strata dip inward toward a trough), with the long axis parallel to the fault. Further west, the folding is anticlinal (upfolding of beds into arches so the beds incline away from the crest on either side) as in the valleys of the Bow and Mistaya rivers, where erosion has worn away the centre of the anticline. The peaks of the Main Ranges of Precambrian and Cambrian rocks during the Castle Mountain Thrust rode up and over late Palaeozoic and Mesozoic rocks, and are quartzites, massive limestone and dolomites.

Alpine glaciation, which is constant, is caused by local climatic conditions. Continental glaciation has occurred four times during the Pleistocene, the geologic era in which man rose to predominance. The trigger of Continental glaciation has not been precisely determined but for some reason the climate of North America cooled. Snow fell and there was very little or no melt. As a result of the constant snowfall and the heavy pressure caused by its own weight, the snow compressed and ice formed; as the ice accumulated glaciers were formed. The weight of the ice forced it to flow down previous river valleys, over cliffs, into gorges. Rocks and boulders were ground and carried along, at the sides and underneath. Glacier flowed into glacier – great ice fields were formed – and in time the Cordilleran Ice Sheet 1200 miles long and 400 miles wide covered Western Canada and part of the United States, only one of three ice sheets on North America. Four successive ice sheets and four periods of recession and warming occurred over millions of years. Only the highest of the rock masses were left visible in this great wasteland of ice and snow. We see remnants of the Ice Age today in our glaciers, near and on the Continental Divide and in the great ice fields; the Columbia Ice Field, on the Banff-Jasper Highway, is one of many. From the highway we often see only the tongues of glaciers such as the Peyto, Yoho and Bow.

Other evidence of the Ice Age is left in the terraces of lateral moraines along the Bow River, one such being just below the Tunnel Mountain campgrounds by the Hoodoos. These queer formations are themselves made from the glacial till of mud and sorted stones cemented together by pressure. The Bow River cut its post-glacial course through the glacial drift left on the valley floor. Entering this main valley are many tributary valleys to be seen high on the mountains today. In them glaciers were left when the ice retreated, which, as they melted, cut the valleys deeper with the water flowing into the Bow River. Terraces were formed from the melt waters and streams of these glaciers, cutting into the drift from the main glacier, as seen on Whitehorn Mountain at Lake Louise. The road to Moraine Lake is along a hanging valley left there by the glacier. Amphitheatres were formed, such as the one on the northwest side of Cascade Mountain.

Cirques (bowl-shaped depressions), caused by the grinding of the ice, are numerous. A beautiful one at the north side of Castle Mountain has two delightful lakes in it. Many may be seen along the Banff-Jasper Highway, some still partially filled with glaciers. Mount Assiniboine, at the headwaters of the Spray, Cross and Simpson rivers, shows how glaciers sculptured cirques into the mountain mass, leaving the resultant pyramid to tower 11,890 feet above sea level. Knife-edged mountains, such as the Kaufmann Peaks on the Banff-Jasper Highway, result from the grinding of a landmass on two sides by two glaciers.

In Lake Minnewanka and Lake Louise, we see examples of lakes formed because the courses of the melt waters were restricted by moraines. Through the Canmore area glacial fans spread at valley outlets. Many of the mountains show the wearing effects of glaciers on their long smooth western slopes (Rundle) as contrasted with the rugged, steep cliffs on the eastern faces. The Bow Valley, once V-shaped, was worn by glacial action, as was the Mistaya River Valley, along the Banff-Jasper Highway. Now both are U-shaped.

The Rocky Mountains are much lower and certainly changed in shape from the great mountain masses thrust up before the Ice Age, but factors other than glaciers enter into the picture as well. Rain, snow, ice, frost, wind, avalanches, landslides, earthquakes and rivers have all played their part in the tearing down and shaping of the mountains. Castle Mountain is an example where the softer shale and slate have eroded, leaving the vertical steps alternating with sloping terraces of the harder quartzites, massive limestone and sandstone. Likewise, Cascade Mountain and Pilot Mountain show this post-glacial erosion.

The Sawback Range, originally a great arch, has been eroded into rows of mountains like sawteeth.

The reptiles were destroyed during the period of the Rocky Mountain formation, when the inland sea was driven back and the swamp growth disappeared. The Ice Age drove the mammals of the early Cenozoic Era out and destroyed forests and flowers. The seeds of the trees and flowers were caught in the ice and scattered; after the melt, when the climate moderated and water began to flow once again, the forests, plants, animals, insects, birds and fish came back to give life to the world after the long desolation. Yet change is still going on; the mountains continue to be worn down and the sediments still go to the ocean bed.

2
EVOLUTION OF THE MOUNTAINS

This brief outline of geological forms has been given so you might understand the history of the Rocky Mountain Region, which we can summarize as follows.

A land mass must be presumed, because of the sediments which were laid down in the great inland seas. The weight of the sediments themselves transformed them to rock. Gradually the rock mass was thrust above the sea and became a large land area covering much of the region. This land remained through the Precambrian period into the middle of the Carboniferous (Mississippian), eroded by the atmosphere and the rivers which carried the sediment to the inland sea covering the area where the Rockies and Selkirks lie today. Many strata, over a long period of time were laid down, and the floor sank under its own weight. The shores changed because of disturbances in the earth's crust but the inland sea still remained.

By the beginning of Pennsylvanian, the land began to sink in the west, and once more, southern British Columbia was inundated by the inland sea. During the Permian and the Triassic, land rose and the sea withdrew, except from the eastern Rocky Mountain and Interior Plateau Regions. During the Jurassic period many disturbances occurred in the earth's crust along the Pacific Coast; though once again, the Rocky Mountain Region remained as before and sedimentation continued in the inland sea. This sea spread in Cretaceous times to cover the Great Plains; sandstones and shales as well as coal, which had formed from the vegetation, were laid down.

By the end of the Cretaceous period, there had been many thrusts and pressures from the west and, for the first time since the Precambrian, it affected the Rocky Mountains. The strata were arched upward, compressed and overturned on each other, and many of the unfolded parts were pushed on the plains. (You may have noticed as you entered them how suddenly the mountains rise.)

By the end of the Tertiary period, the mountains were formed, but it had been a very long slow process. Then began the erosion through development of river systems; and some sedimentary rocks were laid down on the eastern side of the mountains. There still was volcanic action in the west near the Pacific which continued through Tertiary times and into the Quaternary.

The Glacial period which followed changed and shaped the mountain mass extensively and left many deposits. The Tertiary are our youngest consolidated rocks and through Quaternary we only have loose and partially consolidated rocks of the glacial and post-glacial deposits.

3
WATERSHEDS

The Bow River, today, shows an unusual course. It follows a line parallel to the mountains from its source at Bow Summit, to six or seven miles west of Banff, where it turns eastward across the mountain ridges to cross the valley. At Banff, it abruptly turns southeast and cuts through rock walls to plunge over Bow Falls. There it turns northeast, to flow between Rundle Mountain, on the southeast, and Tunnel Mountain on the northwest. After two miles, it turns southeast and continues out of the Park.

Very likely, in pre-glacial times the Bow flowed southeastward, then northeastward through the valley of the present Cascade River and the present Minnewanka Valley, to the plains. The Ice Age brought much debris into all the old valley bottoms and as the glaciers retreated, they left a great mass at the entrance to the old Bow Valley (Cascade) so the new Bow was forced to flow southeastward to join the Old Bow. Very likely, a lake formed in Bow Valley which finally eroded an outlet in the rock wall between Rundle and Tunnel. As the years passed, this barrier was cut down to the limestone ridge it is today.

As the glacier stagnated in the Old Bow Valley, Devil's Lake (Minnewanka) was formed, which drained through Devil's Canyon to the Bow River. Dams built by man add to the confusion. A hydroelectric dam at the west end of Lake Minnewanka raised it sixty to seventy feet. Another diversion channel at the headwaters of the Ghost River, nearly adjacent to the east end of Lake Minnewanka, diverted the Ghost into the Bow farther east.

In the Spray Valley, glacial debris closed it, causing a very large lake to form. Over thousands of years, the Spray eroded a passage through and drained the lake, leaving Upper and Lower Spray Lakes, with some pools and a stream between them. Now a dam across the Spray River Canyon has once again created an enormous lake in the old bed. This dam diverts the water east, to follow its old Goat Creek course, and a lower dam diverts it along a canal and into the Bow.

II

Climate
and Vegetation

The Climate is complicated, because the park is in a western interior location with several mountain ranges between it and the Pacific Coast; because of the latitude, the snowfall is fairly high. The altitude being high, air pressure and air composition are affected. More sunlight comes through; there is less water vapour; and there are fewer impurities or dust. On the other hand, the air is lighter so less heat is held, the calculated loss being three degrees for every 1,000 feet of altitude. During the winter, ninety-five percent of the sun's heat is reflected by the snow, and at night, when the wind lulls, the warm air ascends. Both soil and large lakes absorb heat during the day, both give it off at night. At times, when Continental Polar air from the Arctic meets warm air from the Pacific, Banff will have a temperature inversion because the warm air rides on top of the cold air mass.

The town site lies on the fringe of the Chinook Belt, which means strong west winds can raise the temperature from far below freezing to well above in two or three hours and the snow disappears. The air in a Chinook ascends on the windward side of the mountains and loses its moisture as rain in summer or snow in winter, hence the heavy vegetation found on the west side of the Continental Divide. When it reaches the leeward slope, the Chinook is a dry wind, gaining heat as it loses its humidity and as it loses elevation, which explains the sudden rise in temperature in a few hours and the rapid disappearance of snow along the Bow Valley. In Banff, the Chinook can break a cold spell instantly, and it is a boon to the big ranches on the prairie, where little snow will be left on the ground near the Bow after it has passed.

This strange wind, of course, has led to many tall tales. One man claimed he had to run his horses to Calgary, because he had started out in a sleigh at Morley, and in an hour he could hardly keep ahead of bare ground. Another man said he tied his team to a post, and when he came back in an hour, he found the horses clinging to the church roof. In all these stories, there is some truth.

It is these variations of climate that help to make Banff a favoured resort. In winter the cold dry air produces excellent powder snow. In summer the moderately warm temperatures and low humidity add to the enjoyment of all sports enthusiasts. Both summer and winter conditions promote good health, and many invalids over the years have enjoyed and benefited from the favourable climate.

Vegetation and climate are intimately related. In the sixteenth and seventeenth centuries the glaciers advanced briefly with the subsequent recession starting in the seventeenth century. The retreat continued in the eighteenth and nineteenth centuries except for a brief period of advance in the 1840s and a very minor growth at the turn of the twentieth century. So, generally from 1775 to 1940 the climate was relatively warm and dry. From 1830 to 1900 there was above average precipitation and from 1900 to the 1930s a decline in precipitation and an increase in temperature occurred. Since the 1940s there has been an increase in precipitation and a lowered annual mean temperature.

These changes were deduced from fossil-pollen studies, measurements of glacial movement, analysis of meteorological reports, and tree-ring growth analysis. The study of tree rings of Douglas Fir, Lodgepole Pine and White Spruce showed more precipitation between 1830 and 1900 and less heat; then, until the late 1930s, less moisture and more heat. Meteorological reports kept in Banff from 1895 through the 1930s confirm these trends.

This climatic change was reflected in the change of vegetation. In the cool, moist periods Lodgepole Pine, Spruce and Alpine Fir predominate; in the warmer, drier times the Douglas Fir succeeds and near the Continental Divide even some Lyall's Larch. Among deciduous trees, Aspen Poplar was most constant.

With the warmer drier climate there was an increase in forest fires started by electrical storms. A study of charcoal layers, in the earth, showed fires were plentiful before the time of the white man. Later, travellers, explorers, surveyors and geologists commented on whole valleys of burnt timber. Indians may have accidentally started them with smudge fires, signal fires or campfires. James Hector mentioned that Indians started fires on the prairie to drive the buffalo. But in the mountains it was not likely, because escape from fire was not easy, and a forest fire would mean the destruction of the wild life, on which their own lives depended. With the coming of the white man forest fires increased. He brought the railways, and locomotive sparks caused many fires. His carelessness in camping during the dry period of the summer easily caused fires.

Man, however, must not be blamed for all the destruction of the forests. The hot dry seasons for some years increased fires started by lightning.

Avalanches and landslides swept large areas clear of trees. The white man introduced logging, and great timber companies began exploiting the forests (and still do), but in the National Parks it was soon controlled. Nature provides its own enemies to forests in blights, insects, animals and rodents. To offset his earlier destruction, man very early started protection of forests against fire and logging. Reforestation followed and attempted to control the disease of trees.

Today, broadly speaking, there are in the Rockies areas of tundra, coniferous forest and grassland. The upper tree line at about 7,000 feet above sea level is generally cold, exposed and has steep gradients and little or poor soil. The lower tree line with the same weather has more variable factors in fires, deep snow, wind and slides. At Arctic level snow is permanent. The Alpine tundra, with rock and little moisture is the home of lichens and other primitive vegetation. Below the cliffs are the alpine flowers of arctic and subarctic species, usually low plants, perennials showing rapid seed production or suckering root systems. The rock is porous, and there is little soil and little moisture. The Lyall's Larch stands between the tundra and the coniferous forest. This larch (tamarack) is found between 6,000 and 7,000 feet and may form the tree limit (Sulphur Mountain), may grow in open stands (Larch Valley, Moraine Lake) or may be mixed with Alpine Fir, Englemann Spruce, Mountain Hemlock and Whitebark Pine. The larch is a small tree, thick limbed, with needle-shaped, long soft leaves of a pale bluish green that turn yellow-green before falling in the autumn. The needles are in clusters on the whitish woolly twigs, which become black with age. In contrast, the Western Larch is tall and stately and of an even shape but is found more often across the Continental Divide and more southerly than Banff.

In the Sub-Alpine Zone we find Alpine Fir, Englemann Spruce and on more arid slopes Whitebark Pine, which seldom grow as low as 5,000 feet. The Limber Pine likes drier slopes and little competition; it has an altitude range from 3,000 to 6,000 feet. In the Montane level, roughly 4,700 feet to the valley floor, White Spruce, Balsam Fir, some Limber Pine, Western Hemlock, Rocky Mountain Douglas Fir and Lodgepole Pine are the conifers. The Lodgepole Pine is the most dominant probably because its serotinous (late-forming) cones are capable of withstanding extreme heat and extreme cold.

Among deciduous trees are Balm-of-Gilead, Black Cottonwood, Pussy Willows and Aspen Poplar. The Aspen because of its suckering root system is more impervious to killing; it, like the Lodgepole Pine, comes back first after forest fires. Generally speaking Spruce is the dominant species and will replace all others over some two hundred years, only, so some authorities claim, to be replaced by Fir.

On well-drained terraces of fire-burnt areas there is little tree growth, more grass, juniper shrubs and low bushes such as raspberry, bearberry or

Snow Lily

strawberry plants. Beaver dams may cause flood plain conditions with willows, low birch, sedges and grass and some herbaceous plants such as mint or cress. Avalanches and landslides also produce shrub areas.

In the mountains, stable grasslands are to be found where rough fescue predominates, with such flowers as the low forget-me-nots and others that like sun. If such areas are grazed they produce fescue and June grass and some sedges. The Kootenay Plain and the Yah-Ha-Tinda are two such places in the mountains.

One who does not live here can scarcely realize the variety and beauty of the different flowers at different seasons, nor the succession of their blooming times. For instance some species which bloom early in the valley bottoms will be found in bloom a month later at higher levels. The early flowers of the high altitude species belong there and only bloom there.

From the alpine meadows through the open forest or park areas, to the shady swamp areas, to the open meadow, one may find flowers of many varieties: the yellow violets in their shady nooks, the Calypso, the daintiest of the orchids, growing in shady mossy spots, and its bigger cousins, the white and yellow Lady's Slippers, growing in wet spots; the true Forget-me-not, on grassy slopes or meadows, are very beautiful. The reddish-orange Western

Wood Lily grows in the lower river valleys and on the edges of woods in early July, while the bright yellow Snow Lily appears immediately after the snow melts, to last but a short time on the slides and mountain slopes at 5,000 feet or higher. The Iris family has familiar representatives in the Violet, and the Blue-eyed grass which blooms in June, on open moist ground. The Pasque flower heralds spring, blooming in May and June, depending on the location and it is frequently called the crocus which it resembles. By the roadsides one sees the Wild Rose and in shadier ground the Mountain Avens.

When the summer is stretching out, the Columbines, Anemones, Clematis and Buttercups are gone, then come the Gaillardia, Purple Asters, the Pearly Everlasting, the false Heathers and the red Indian Paint (or Painter's) Brush or in the high altitude meadows the white or yellow Indian Paint Brush.

The many flowering shrubs include among others Chokecherry, High Bush Cranberry, Baneberry, Raspberry, Honeysuckle and Labrador Tea.

III

Wildlife in Rocky Mountains Park

1
MAMMALS

The early explorers and travellers in the country that would become the Park commented on the animals they used for food or hunted for trophies. Before them, the Indians hunted not only for the food but for the hides which were used for tipis and clothes.

After the Ice Age the mammals became predominant. On the rock slopes of the high Alpine Zone you will hear a distinctive squeak or whistle from the Pika or "rock rabbit" which is only six to eight inches in size. Coming lower to the Montane, one may find the Snowshoe Hare, thirteen to eighteen inches, dark brown in summer, turning white in winter.

Of the gnawing animals there are the Beavers in lakes and streams. At Vermilion Lakes, one sees many of their houses, and in the evening the canoeist, on the Bow, will hear the loud slap of their tails. Muskrats also live in these lakes and, in the winter, may be seen swimming beneath the ice. Both the young beavers and the young muskrats like to slide down mud slopes into the water. The Porcupine lives in the forest and is most active at night. This inoffensive animal, active in a tree, is unfortunately, slow on the ground, and is frequently the victim of automobiles. His quills will come out only when grasped.

The Golden Mantle Ground Squirrel is marked and coloured like a chipmunk. He begins to hibernate from September. He is found at higher altitudes than the Columbian Ground Squirrel which one sees in most open areas. People mistakenly call him a "gopher". The Marmot or Siffleur (French meaning "whistler") is well known for his shrill call and his yellow-grey body. He, too, hibernates. The mischievous Red Squirrel, seven to eight inches, nests in tree trunks, at the base of which one frequently sees piles of cone scales.

Wapiti

He and the various striped chipmunks are numerous. The Northern Flying Squirrel may be seen at night along Spray Avenue on Sulphur Mountain.

The following ungulates are indigenous to the park. The Mule Deer is seen around Banff with his even, pronged antlers, which he sheds yearly. The White Tail Deer, which is seldom seen now, may be recognized by his tail which he holds upright when he bounds away. The prongs of his antlers come from a main beam on either side. The Black Tail Deer, though mentioned by early explorers, is no longer found in this area, having migrated to the United States.

The Rocky Mountain Sheep or Big Horn have massive curled horns and are brown in colour. They are most frequently seen on grass slopes or along the highways. In the summer the males generally herd together, separated from the females. The Mountain Goat, white with black horns, ranges higher than the sheep (Rundle Mountain), though at times they are seen near a highway (Banff-Jasper Highway).

Moose are dark brown with heavy flat antlers. In the summer they live around lakes, as they feed on water vegetation; in the winter they eat woody plants. The Moose has a bell-shaped tuft of fur below his jaw depending on its age. He appears awkward compared with Wapiti or Deer but can move as rapidly on land and in the water. The Woodland Caribou are sleek, deep biscuit in colour, with large antlers. These animals are very shy and are now seen only at high altitudes along the Banff-Jasper Highway, the Pipestone River and in Palliser Pass as well as along the Great Divide from Banff to Mount Robson.

In early times the Wood Bison, hunted by the Indians, were found in the area – in valleys, along rivers, and even on summits – but they are found no longer. Early explorers have written about them on Simpson Pass and Athabasca Pass. Today buffalo are either privately owned or in game preserves.

Of the flesh-eating animals, the Black Bear is most frequently seen. He averages 300 to 500 pounds and has a longer head and more pointed nose than the Grizzly. The Black Bear's colour ranges from black through brown to almost white. He semi-hibernates depending on the weather. The Grizzly or Silvertip, as he is often called because his brown hair has light tips, has a hump behind his shoulders. His face is broad and flat and his small eyes very near-sighted, for which he is compensated by his keen sense of smell. For all his lumbering appearance he can run up to thirty miles an hour.

Coyotes are numerous and, at night, come into town. They are beige-brown with black markings and run with their bushy tails straight out. They eat rodents and rabbits and weigh twenty five to thirty pounds. The Gray Wolf weighs seventy to one hundred twenty pounds and resembles a large dog. He runs with his tail held high. The value of wolves in helping to keep the balance of nature is now recognized, so they are gradually increasing in number in remote valleys such as the Clearwater.

The Mountain Lion or Cougar is sleek, and light brown in colour. Like the Lynx or Bob Cat, which is grey with some black, their range is Cascade, Tunnel or Stony Squaw Mountains near Banff. They are generally shy, dangerous only if molested or startled.

Wolverines are not often seen around Banff any more, though they are found at Lake Louise. They average thirty-five to fifty pounds. Of the same family are the Skunks and Weasels, both of which are fairly widespread in the area. In the winter, the Weasel turns from brown to white with a black tip on his tail, and is known in the fur trade as "ermine". Marten, the sable of the fur trade, still exist in fairly large numbers in the more remote valleys.

Generally, wild animals are not dangerous if left alone, unless they are sick, or fear for their young. It is always wise to respect them and not ask for trouble – and never to forget they are wild.

The Wapiti, or Red Deer *(Cervus Canadensis Nelsoni)* commonly called Elk is not indigenous to Banff National Park. Considering the numbers one sees now, their history is interesting. David McDougall said he had killed Wapiti when he came to Old House Lake (Jacob Lake) just north of Morley, but they were gone, or nearly so, by the late 1800s. Later John Englishman, a Stony at Morley, said he had killed them north of Morley; and Peter Wesley, another Stony, said he had once shot one south of there. These men were speaking of the early 1870s and early 1880s. The Indians said they were 'all gone'; after 'very cold winter, many die'. Michase, a Cree, confirmed these reports by saying he killed them northwest of Morley near the mountains when he was a young man. One day when Jim Simpson and I were talking about Sir George Simpson's trip, I said he had spoken of one of his men killing a Red Deer near the Bow Traverse and asked Jim Simpson if he had ever seen any Wapiti in the Park in the early days. He told me he could not remember any before they were brought in by the government and said it was possible the odd animal might have drifted over the passes, but even in British Columbia he did not remember seeing too many. Norman Luxton, who also did a lot of hunting, told me he had not seen any before the government planted them in the park. A study of the writings of the early travellers in this area showed mention of some of the other animals but not the Red Deer. The severe winters in the 1890s must have destroyed the Wapiti east of the Rockies either because of the cold or resultant weakening so they succumbed to disease.

In 1916, the Park authorities negotiated with the National Park Service of United States, and, in 1917, fifty-seven Wapiti came from Yellowstone National Park as a result. They were not turned out to forage for themselves until June of the following year. In 1919 and 1920, over three hundred more Wapiti came from Yellowstone and some fifty were turned out at Massive, over two hundred in the Bow Valley and over a hundred at Duthill. The wardens watched their migration and Wapiti were reported in the Panther River area by 1927, and the Yah-Ha-Tinda by 1933, the Clearwater in 1942 and the Little Pipestone where they wintered in 1942-43. They multiplied rapidly and, in the 1930s, there were great numbers along the Bow from the Park entrance to Lake Louise, and up the Spray and Cascade Valleys. By 1943 it was necessary to kill the surplus and each winter since many have been removed.

This importing of Wapiti has badly upset the balance of nature in the flora and fauna of the Park. Everything favoured the Wapiti. Their first winter they were turned out on the summer range of the sheep, deer, moose and beaver, also they were in areas where few predators were left. In 1935, cougars had been systematically killed by Park rulings, and, unfortunately wolves had always been controlled. The Wapiti is greedy and versatile and will eat grass or browse on willows and aspen. These foods grow in areas produced mainly by forest fires and to a lesser extent by avalanches or landslides. Here again man has changed the pattern by greater control of forest fires. The Wapiti themselves spoil good grazing in upper valley areas because their hooves tear the sod and erosion carries away the 'never abundant' soil.

In the 1920s, the Beaver were very plentiful in the Vermilion Lake area, then as there were no more trees, they retreated up the Bow and to Forty Mile Creek where there were more predators. Hundreds of Bighorn Sheep used to be just west of Banff; now they are disappearing because the Wapiti are forcing them into the marginal area of food supply as they are mainly grazers. Deer are browsers, though they will graze if forced to, but the Wapiti are eating the Willows and Aspen so fast that the latter is disappearing from the area. In time, no doubt, the Deer will be crowded out. Up to the present the Moose have been least affected, but if the Wapiti start to crowd the swamp areas the Moose will change their migration pattern. There was a time when Moose used to be plentiful in the meadows west of Johnston Canyon, but, now, not one is seen.

There is no doubt that early hunting in the Park and construction of roads and trails brought about change in migratory habits of some of the animals. Sheep, Deer, Moose and Bears seem to show little reaction to this, even Goats stayed much the same in number until the late 1920s. Now, with more car travel, Goats have moved into the higher altitudes.

2
BIRDS

Banff area is very fortunate in having many species of birds, but, like the flowers, many of them are shy and stay in the woods. Birdwatching is a favourite hobby of many, and the Park is a very beautiful place for it.

Most of the following birds are readily seen along trails and in campsites. The Magpie is a fairly large bird with iridescent black feathers and white bars on the shoulders, and a very long tail. Like the Crow he stays all winter. Ravens are very black and larger than Crows, and have come only within the last three years to Banff. The Grey Jay, or Whisky Jack, is grey with a white vest and head, about robin size. The Clark's Crow or Nutcracker is larger, grey with white tail feathers, black on the wings and a long beak. The Steller's or Mountain Jay is very handsome, crested, dark blue with touches of black. He is smaller than the lighter-coloured Blue Jay, not found here.

The Oregon Junco is slate and brownish with a black head. The Slate Junco has a lighter breast. Both may be identified by the white outer tail feathers. The Chicadee, who cheerily calls his name, is brownish with a black cap and a white ring on his neck. The Mountain Chicadee has a white line over his eye and is a dull orange colour. The pretty, dark blue Bank Swallows nest in colonies in the banks of rivers or streams. Any summer evening one may see hundreds of them cutting figures in the sky. The Mountain Bluebird with its sweet song is very shy, unlike its Eastern cousin; its breast is blue. Since Banff has become busier these birds stay more to the bush, though some still nest in town. Our Western Robin is a welcome sight with his rusty red breast and greyish brown back and black head and wings. His 'chur-up' can do much for a dull day; besides, his liking for worms helps the gardener. Downy, the smallest woodpecker, is black and white with a red spot on his head. Hairy Woodpecker is similar but a little larger. The Red-Breasted Nuthatch is more often seen in winter or spring and has a white line over his eye and a very pointed beak. Cedar and Bohemian Wax Wings come through in the spring and fall. They are a beautiful beige with darker markings and are crested.

Early explorers, travellers and settlers were interested in the game birds as an additional source of food. Ruffed grouse are still found in the woods. These birds were easily killed because, even if one or more of the flock were killed by hunters throwing stones, the others did not fly; so they were called Fool-Hens. Ptarmigan in the summer are brown and white and black, but in winter turn white with black markings; they are a fine example of protective colouration.

The Common Loon, larger than a duck and with a shorter neck than a swan, sends its weird cry over lake waters. Their even white bars over the back, black head, neck and beak identify them readily. Various ducks, Mallards, Mergansers, Canvas-Backs, Pin Tail, Blue Wing and Green Wing Teal stop at the lakes while migrating, and some stay to breed. As there is a warm sulphur spring that comes into the one lake, ducks often winter there, where the water does not freeze.

The Whistling Swans, large white birds with touches of grey, stop every spring and fall at Vermilion lakes when migrating. The Osprey, large, brown and white, nests at the lakes. Canada Geese stop spring and fall when migrating.

Golden Eagles are found on this side of the Continental Divide and may be distinguished by the feathers on their legs. The Bald Headed Eagle, after four years when he reaches maturity, has a white head and tail. He is a great fisher, and may be seen around the lakes.

3
FISH

Many tall tales have been told around the camp fires or in front of the fireplaces about the fish that were lost. Such was the quantity of fish in the early days that even these stories could be true. Lake Minnewanka, from the time of the first fishermen to the recent hopeful ones, has yielded thirty-pound lake trout. The smaller ice cold lakes have always had plenty of Cutthroat, Rainbow and Dolly Varden Trout. Camping parties go up the Spray or to Twin lakes and many others to fish. The first white men depended on fresh fish for a meal if their supplies ran out when they were exploring, surveying or climbing. In those days, one caught as many fish as there were hooks on a line; today, one works a little harder, but the fish are still there. The government has for many years stocked rivers, streams and lakes. In early days many people fished through the ice. Later, the practice was forbidden for a number of years. In 1973, ice-fishing again became legal on the Bow River, although night-lines are forbidden.

When the Rocky Mountains Park started, no fishing permits were required. After automobiles were allowed, a free license to fish came with the car permit. Other people could obtain one at the Park Superintendent's office. Then came the time (as now) when fishing permits had to be purchased. Seldom does one go to below the Bow Falls without seeing several anglers in their favourite spots.

Before the caves at the Middle Springs were sealed by government order, many people used to go there to see the prehistoric fish. These white translucent fish, about the size of minnows, lived in the warm sulphur water in the caves, and were a real attraction for visitors.

IV

The First
Mountain People

The North American Indian has been much mentioned, either idealized or damned. People do not realize he was simply a human being living under difficult conditions. He may have been savage and brutal, but he had to be, or die. His inscrutable stoicism before other men was only a mask to hide his feelings or pain. Of courage, he had plenty; of pride, he had too much; of kindness, he had sufficient for his women and children, and he would look after the sick or wounded. Since the Indians were the first men we know to penetrate the Rocky Mountain area, and to travel it continuously, it is important to establish who they were and what their lifestyle was.

Of the Indians, before the explorers came, we know little. Only through their own stories, which have been handed down by word of mouth, can we learn something of those days. Their Medicine Men told of creation by Manitou, or the Great Spirit, an all powerful god. They foretold, also, the coming of the whiteman, or 'Sky Being' as they called him; likewise the horse, or 'Sky Dog'. The Indians believed that with their coming, all work would be done and life would be wonderful. From Indian lore we learn of nations at war, of feuds, of hunting and of epidemics, all before the white men came.

For our knowledge of the very early times, comparatively speaking, we have to depend on accounts of the explorers and fur traders. Anthony Henday, who lived with the Indians in 1754 and 1755, seems to have appreciated their good qualities; however, David Thompson, a perceptive observer, gives us a better picture in his Journals, where he describes them at length and with understanding. It is only in recent times, less than a hundred years, that linguists and ethnologists have been able to tell us about the differences and the relationships of the Indian tribes and languages.

The Assiniboine or Stony Indians were represented in this area, and were a branch of the Siouan nation. The early explorers said the Assiniboine country extended from the Red River to the confluence of the North and

South Saskatchewan Rivers. They were gradually pushed westward by the Blackfoot, until the area of the Rocky Mountains Park to Jasper Park and the adjoining foothills became their territory. The name 'Stony' comes from the fact that they used hot stones in their hide bags to heat water and cook food.

The Blackfoot are of Algonkian origin and were for many years the rulers of the plains. Their territory extended from the headwaters of the Missouri to the Saskatchewan and from the Red River west to the Rocky Mountains. They had three bands: the Siksika or Blackfoot proper, so called, because their moccasin soles were always black; the Blood; and the Piegan. Legend says they descended from three brothers, so belonged to one family. In early times, they probably migrated from the east, breaking away from the Algonkians. Being numerous, warlike and strong, they forced other Indians of the plains, such as the Stonys, to retreat to the hills and mountains.

The Sarsi originally belong to the Beaver tribe of the Athapascans. When the Sarsi took their name and migrated south, they became allies of the Blackfoot, but kept their own customs and language.

The Cree tribes are Algonkians, like the Blackfoot, but have a different dialect. They originally had territory extending from Hudson's Bay and Athabasca Lake to the Rocky Mountains. Being warlike they invaded Blackfoot and Athapascan territories. The Assiniboine (Stony) and Cree became allies against the Blackfoot. We hear of battles they fought from Indian legends and early explorers.

The Kootenay, according to legend, were a nation near present day Fort Macleod. They lived east of the mountains, hunted buffalo and traded with the Assiniboine. The Blackfoot and early epidemics drove half of them across the mountains and they became the Kootenay. Today the Lower Kootenay tribe is on the eastern boundary of Waterton National Park in Alberta and the Upper Kootenay is in the area of Upper Kootenay River.

The Shuswap, a tribe of the Salish, originally had the area between Jasper Park, at the headwaters of the Athabasca, and the Fraser Rivers. Now they are near Arrow Lake, south of Revelstoke Park, though before that they were at Shuswap Lake.

Today the Stony Indians have a reserve at Morley, midway between Banff and Calgary, and a small one at Eden Valley in the Highwood River area. The Sarsi reserve is near Calgary. At Gleichen, about fifty miles east of Calgary, is the Blackfoot reserve and the Piegan are at Brocket, east of Pincher Creek on the Crow's Nest Pass railway. The Blood have the largest reserve in Canada on the Oldman River near Fort Macleod.

All these tribes were nomadic people, their tipis and few possessions easy to move. The buffalo supplied all their needs, food, tipis, clothes, moccasins and robes. Originally, the Indians hunted buffalo on foot with bows and arrows. They crawled singly to the edges of the herd and shot the animals as they grazed. Sometimes Indians, covered with buffalo robes, acted as decoys.

Norman Luxton with William Hunter Snr, a Stony, circa 1939.

They called like calves to bring the cows close, which other Indians would kill. After horses came, there was the running hunt, where the Indian killed from horseback. Other times a large group of Indians would stampede the buffalo over cliffs or high river banks. Some animals died in the fall or were trampled by others, and Indians at the bottom killed incapacitated animals. Though popular, it was a wasteful way to kill. Such jumps in the vicinity of the Rockies were at Jumping Pound, west of Calgary; one west of Cayley, and another west of Fort Macleod.

One does not think of plains buffalo as being in the mountain region, but David McDougall saw a small number around Devil's Head Mountain in the 1870s. These continued to range in that area until the Stonys and Crees killed them after the numerous herds had disappeared from the plains. Plains Indians did not like fowl or fish, and in some tribes, such as the Blackfoot, fish was taboo. In the 1800s half-starved Stonys and Crees hunted in the mountains and killed mountain sheep, deer, moose, mountain goat and Wood caribou.

All tribes, in early times, fought to keep their own territory, because there they were free to roam and hunt in safety. Few pitched battles were fought because they had only primitive weapons, the stone tomahawk and flint arrowheads. Because of such weapons not too many died in battle. Only after the advent of the white man and the flintlock, did large numbers of both Indians and animals die in battle and the hunt. Explorers and traders tell of pitched battles between the Cree and Blackfoot. The fur trade also caused hatred between the Piegan and the Kootenay. Sometimes the trade was dangerous even for white men as we hear from incidents in David Thompson's journeys.

For many years Kootenay Plain, near the headwaters of the North Saskatchewan, had been a trading ground for the fur companies and the Kootenay, who crossed the mountains. The location was good for the Kootenay, with an easy escape route to their homes. However, as early as 1807, the North West Company post at Kootenay Plain was forced to close because the Blackfoot had guns. For many years, the Blackfoot dominated both Indian and white man, but smallpox and scarlet fever killed thousands of them, as these epidemics did among all the tribes. By 1845, the Crees to the east, the Crows to the south and the Flatheads in the west were breaking Blackfoot power.

The first white explorers, Henday and Thompson, reported that the Indians had horses. Thompson wrote that an old chief told him they had stolen their horses in the 1720s or 1730s from their enemies, the Snake Indians, who came from the west side of the mountains. Horse stealing was honourable and the tribes would send out small parties of braves to do just that.

Each tribe had its own chiefs and councillors in the different bands into which a tribe was divided. Each tribe had its military (braves), its police, and its societies, some of which were secret, for men and for women. Many of the societies had Medicine Bundles, which were cared for with much ceremony. Each Indian had his own 'Good Medicine', which might be any animal seen in a dream, or a stone, or a piece of bark or skin.

Despite their common devotion to the horse and the buffalo hunt, the Indians in and on the borders of the mountains differed in their life styles. The Blackfoot and Sarsi were polygamous, which posed a problem for the missionary at a much later date. One old chief said of his wives, "How can I choose when I love them all?"

Thompson writes that the Piegan had a hard life. From earliest childhood, they were taught to use the bow for protection against enemies and starvation. In the Piegan tribe the chiefs descended through one family; a chiefdom was not elective as in other tribes. The chief had scouts to report to him where the buffalo were, and it was the chief's duty to go around to all the tipis and report all he had heard and to advise. The war chief was more powerful and more respected by the tribe, when on a war party. He would camp by himself, a day closer to the Snakes, to show this bravery.

The Piegan were tall, muscular and had intelligent faces, large black eyes, straight noses, good teeth and long, black straight hair. The men wore long, skin leggings stretching from the ground to their breasts, secured by a belt of skin. The women wore long, straight dresses of skin from shoulder to feet. Their ornaments were bear-claw or deer-tooth necklaces, and both men and women wrapped themselves in buffalo robes.

Marriages were arranged by female relatives of the man and the woman. If the girl decided she did not want to be a fifth wife of an old man, she might elope with the one she loved. If, however, the pair were caught, he was killed and she had her nose cut off; if they were not caught, a settlement could be made for a price, even as it could be when a horse was stolen. Adultery was punishable by death. Public insults were not to be tolerated and were avenged even to death. Thompson witnessed an incident in camp, when a man in a temper flicked his wife with a whip. Shortly after, she came from the tipi where she had retired, told her husband he had shamed her before the tribe, and, drawing a knife, stabbed herself in the breast.

All the tribes believed in a Great Spirit, which was kind and controlled the animals and seasons. The Indians might ask for or thank the Great Spirit for good hunting, success in battle and many good horses. Generally, though, they felt they had a sense of self-sufficiency in most of the events of their lives. They believed in a future life in the Happy Hunting Grounds, where all the good things were. Medicine Men were prophets and foretold the outcome of events by interpreting dreams. The dream gave them an out if they were wrong, but if the interpretation proved right the Medicine Men were considered very wise.

All Indians liked gambling, and they all liked guessing games. Of the latter, the favourite was the old one of concealing an object in the hand – then – which hand? The way the Indians played it the game could continue all evening and the next one too.

Alexander Henry, the Younger, had, unlike Thompson, a poor opinion of the Blackfoot. He had no use for their religion or their morals. But, after all, Henry considered them only as possible hunters. He could not understand why the Blackfoot, who hunted sufficiently for their own needs, would not become servants of the North West Company and trap beaver for a few baubles. He admired the physiques of the men and commented on their hair. On the other hand, he said the women were filthy, combed their hair with their fingers when they put red earth in it and were ugly. Thompson, more broadminded, said each race had its own standards of beauty. Later explorers, Butler, Palliser and Hector, confirmed Thompson's impressions.

The Kootenay, when they were driven west across the mountains, adapted very well to their new environment. They still kept some of their earlier customs, of which buffalo hunting was one. To these they added fishing and trapping. The communal type of hunting, trapping and fishing was an adaptation, as were the tipis and snowshoes they used after crossing the mountains.

The Upper Kootenay, who were more dependent on buffalo hunting and closer to the mountain passes, organized the hunt. They invited the Lower Kootenay to participate and often as many as eighty lodges of Kootenay might cross for the hunt. Women and children as well as horses, for hunting and packing, went on the summer and fall hunts. On the January hunt, because of deep snow, the children and horses were left behind.

The June hunt was the largest because the buffalo were close to the mountains then. The winter hunt was carried on with snowshoes. The buffalo were in small scattered groups and it was a harder hunt. Speed in skinning and butchering was essential; to do two carcasses a day was good-going for one person. Carrying two or three loads going back and forth in four weeks was good hard work over the passes. Their snowshoes were rounded for hilly or bushy country and were long with upturned pointed tips for trail or plains use. Little or no pemmican was made by the Kootenay; they cut the meat in strips and dried it by sun and fire.

The Lower Kootenay had deer, moose, mountain sheep, red deer and goats to follow where they lived so the buffalo hunt was not as important. Deer hunting and duck hunting were communal efforts. The Deer Chief from the Lower Kootenay band scouted for game signs on the banks of streams before the fall hunt. He sent invitations to the Upper Kootenay, chose the best area and selected the teams of men and boys.

The Duck Chief studied lines of flight, then barriers were set up parallel to these. A net was stretched across the end of the gap. He had to know exactly how to force a low, leisurely flight, so the birds would become entangled in the net.

Eagles were trapped by digging a pit in which an Indian hid. Light brush covered it and on top of that a dead animal acted as bait. When the eagle landed the Indian grasped one leg and killed the bird with his knife. Eagle feathers, much prized by all Indians, were used in trading with the Plains Indians.

Fishing, another common effort, was done differently at various seasons. The Kootenay hooks were two bones bound together in a V-shape and were attached to Indian hemp lines. These were strung on a line stretched from bank to bank on a river and left overnight. At flood times weirs were built across narrow parts of the river, and when the water fell, the large numbers of fish left in the shallows were speared or clubbed. Naturally, the Fishing Chief was in command. Woven conical traps, often ten feet by three feet with a small inner cone as entrance, were used successfully.

Roots and berries were used as food by all Indians. The Kootenay added the tree hair moss of this environment. It was either baked underground beneath a fire for several days or was dried, pounded, then dampened and made into cakes which were baked. Barks and roots were medicines common to all tribes.

The sturgeon-nosed canoe (pointed at prow and stern) was familiar to the Kootenay, and a contrast to the birch bark canoe of the Cree.

Kootenay clothes for men and women, like those of the Plains Indian, were of hide, but differed because only fringe was used for trim. Even their parfleche bags had fringe trim, longer fringe indicating the more valuable contents. The men wore raw hide brimmed hats in summer, and soft fur ones in the winter. In summer the women wore garlands of willow or Osier as protection from the sun, and as easy identification in the event of a raid. Their moccasins were square-toed and heeled, in contrast to the Stony flat-shoe and the pointed Cree moccasin. Men might wear a single feather stuck in their hair or hatband to indicate their skill as hunters. Some Plains Indians used porcupine quills for trim on clothes and bags. When trade with the whites started the southern tribes used beads in geometrical designs and the northern used silk embroidery in floral designs as well as beads.

All Indians liked to paint their faces and bodies. The Kootenays used the Ochre Beds near Marble Canyon; for yellow, the dried mud was used and for red, they obtained it by burning then drying the mud. These Paint Pots are now accessible by a foot path near Marble Canyon, and are worthy of a visit. This, too, was a commodity for trade. Their four-foot bows of yew or cedar were another article of trade. The bows were curved on either side of the hand grip and points, and were bound with sinew. So desirable were these bows that even a horse would be traded for one.

The Upper Kootenay, like the Plains Indians, used eight or ten buffalo hides for their tipis, but the Lower Kootenay used Red Deer hides or mats of Indian hemp or dogbane. In the winter, they all used A-shaped long houses built on tripod frames, and covered with mats of hide or fibre. The Shuswap dug shallow, circular pits over which the tipis were pitched. There were several of these pits on lower Tunnel Mountain, in earlier days, where flint arrow heads could be found.

By coiling roots and sewing them with root thread the Kootenay made baskets; for carrying baskets or liquid containers they used sewn birch bark. In the latter the bark was folded over, then sewn, and often seams were covered with pitch to make them more leak proof.

The use of the pipe was common to all tribes. Soapstone from the Lower Columbia was used, or they traded for catlinite from the headwaters of the Missouri. As tobacco was considered a gift from the gods, much ceremony accompanied smoking.

Of the Indians in the mountains it is hard to tell much, because we know so little. We know the plains buffalo supplied the needs of food, clothes, robes, shelter and saddles for the Plains Indians. It is likely the Wood Stonys and Crees were more familiar with mountain areas. They hunted for sheep, deer, Wood caribou and Wood buffalo, and goat. Signs of old trails where they had gone and campsites were found in the Saskatchewan River Basin; to and from the Kootenay Plain; and to Lake Minnewanka; up the Bow River; into the Kananaskis and the Spray Valleys. After all, the Indians were the guides for the explorers and showed them how to reach the mountain passes and they would be likely to use familiar trails and camps. Indians had crossed the mountains to steal horses and to wage war, before the white man came. The very old Indians of my great grandfather's day told him stories of such events. In the writings of the explorers, the Indian guide was prominent: James Hector had his Nimrod and Peter Erasmus, A.P. Coleman his Job Beaver, Reverend John McDougall his Jonas Jonas and George Simpson his Peechee.

It was inevitable that the Indian would have some effect on the areas he frequented. He would hunt for sheep again and again in the same place, not giving the herd a chance to replenish itself. Fortunately there were enough animals in other areas so they did not become extinct. The Wood buffalo, however, were almost extinct in the mountains before the time of the white man. The Wood antelope retreated to very high, inaccessible places and were saved from extermination. The Indian did much less damage to wildlife than the white men who were to follow him. Possibly his belief that the Great Spirit would always bring animals back hindered him from any thought of conservation, but he killed only to maintain life.

The destruction of the buffalo was completed by 1879 and 1880, this ended a way of life for the Indian and reduced them to pitiable conditions. Only then would the Indians give up their vast territories to the white man and agree to settle on reservations. The buffalo were gone, the beaver practically gone, the fur trade was ended and by then the Indians had become accustomed to the facilities of the white man. No longer was he self-sufficient and free. He had to accept what he was given though it destroyed his culture and his way of life. His morale was weakened; his religion and even the training of his family were changed. He no longer knew what to believe or how to live. The white man came with his conflicting faiths, his ideas of morals and marriage, and the impact on the Indian was devastating. He no longer could believe in his own faith and the new faith left much to be desired. His ideas of marriage had to change, he no longer taught his son at the age of two the simple tasks or at six the use of weapons, nor taught him as a youth to be brave, strong and withstand torture. The girls still learned household chores and the use of plants but these were complicated by the white man's ideas of friendliness and use; Indian societies still existed but some of their dances were frowned upon and their Medicine Bundles were not understood. The white man did not seem to understand the spirits associated with trees, stones or animals. The Indian had epidemics before the white man ever came – their legends tell of these – but after the white man the Indian suffered from many more diseases and neither their simple remedies nor the Medicine Men could help. The Indian no longer travelled, hunted, fought or built up resistance to disease and starvation by fasting, simple food or feats of strength. Probably the worst enemy they had was firewater, the liquor of the white man.

Today, the Indian is trying to regain his rights and a way of life, but will he ever regain a fraction of his glorious heritage? Today his Medicine Men are disillusioned; they see the evils wrought by the 'Sky Beings' and the destruction of Indian youth. They are trying to bring the Indian back to his faith, his culture, and yet be able to work with white man's training and tools. It is hard to ranch or farm after knowing the freedom of the nomad and the excitement of the hunt. The chiefs no longer have power and the Indian laws and rules seem to have gone. Whether the Medicine Men and the small number of Indians who have acquired the white man's education will be able to bring the sadly depleted people back to a way of life, where they may have the best of both Indian and white cultures and living, remains to be seen.

In more recent years, evidence of an earlier people than the Indians has been found in the area, but, as yet, not enough to draw any conclusions. They may have been part of the same people who made the drawings-on-stone found elsewhere in Alberta.

V

Traders, Travellers and Missionaries

The fur trade was, from first to last, a business enterprise, designed to exploit the Indian and the resources of the West. Business forced the fur companies to explore the hinterland and, finally, to find a route to the Pacific. The traders were dependent on the Indian and took care of him to the extent it suited their own ends. As a result we do not find in Canada bloody battles between white and Indian. The Indian, as guide and hunter, was given food, ammunition and help. Then he was given alcohol, but in the case of the Hudson's Bay Company throughout most of the period after 1820, the liquor was diluted so that the native would not become frenzied. The trader had to protect himself. Whiskey Traders, the renegades of a later era in the West, are not part of this story.

The fur companies established the trails of the West, but discouraged development and settlement as detrimental to their business. However, they opened the way for the trained observers of a later period.

In the beginning it was the French voyageurs who first came west from Canada because of their familiarity with canoe transport and their capacity to get on well with the Indians. Competition between the Hudson's Bay and the North West Company, which developed later, forced the former company to abandon its policy of remaining at its posts on Hudson Bay. Earlier, the policy of encouraging the Indians to bring their furs down to the Bay was the object of Henry Kelsey's and Anthony Henday's inland expeditions.

As early as 1691 and 1692, the eighteen-year-old Kelsey accompanied the Indians inland to live with them and establish good trading relations. His route is hard to trace but it is believed he reached the Touchwood Hills area of Saskatchewan. In his journal, half poetry and half prose, he made notes on the vegetation, thought the prairies barren because there were no trees, and described a buffalo hunt. He was the first European to see the Canadian plains and their great herds of buffalo.

In 1751 Jacques Repentigny Legardeur de Saint-Pierre ordered Chevalier de Niverville to establish a post up the Saskatchewan. Ten men were sent by de Niverville to do so. They said they built Fort Lajonquiere at the foot of the mountains. To this day its location is a mystery; it has been alleged, although without much foundation, that the fort was located somewhere in the vicinity of Calgary.

From 1754 to 1755, the Hudson's Bay Company sent Henday to the plains with Indians who were returning home from trading at Hudson Bay. The object of his journey was to persuade the Blackfoot to go to the Bay to trade. He visited the French post at The Pas and, five days later, left Carrot River near Saskatoon and crossed the plains, which he found barren. By September he was somewhere southwest of Red Deer. He had water problems crossing the plains, which he called *Muscuty*, and he said there were plenty of buffalo in what is now Alberta. It is generally conceded that he saw the mountains, and was the first white man to do so in Canada. Henday did meet and talk to the Blackfoot but they preferred to let other Indians take their furs to the Bay. It was a long, hard, and fruitless trip from the trader's viewpoint.

In 1774, Samuel Hearne was sent by the Hudson's Bay Company to establish Cumberland House on the Saskatchewan, its first fort in the interior. In 1778, Peter Pond, a free trader from Montreal, explored the Beaver River and crossed a portage he called the Methy, which was eleven miles long from Isle a la Crosse Lake to the Clearwater River, a tributary of the Athabasca, which he followed to Lake Athabasca. He, like Alexander Henry, the Elder, also from Montreal, who was in the west in 1775 and 1776, saw the possibility of a route to the Pacific Ocean. Both men had their geography confused, because Pond thought the Mackenzie flowed to the Pacific and Henry confused the Peace and Mackenzie Rivers. Alexander Mackenzie did follow the Mackenzie River to the Arctic in 1789, and in 1793, followed the Peace River through its Pass and along or near the Parsnip, Fraser, Blackwater and Bella Coola Rivers to the Pacific. This was the first crossing of the continent north of Mexico, and occurred ten years before Lewis and Clarke crossed the United States.

In 1785, David Thompson was sent from England, at age fourteen, to serve seven years with the Hudson's Bay Company. In 1787, Thompson was sent from Manchester House to winter with the Piegan on the Bow River and learn their language, and there he saw the mountains for the first time. He was sent to winter, 1789-90, at Cumberland House to recuperate from a broken leg. There Philip Tumor, the surveyor, added to Thompson's knowledge. The following year, his apprenticeship finished, Thompson went to York Factory, where he was under Malcolm Ross from 1792 to 1797. In that year, Thompson told Ross he was going to join the North West Company. His abrupt departure from the Hudson's Bay Company is still unexplained.

In 1798, Thompson wintered at Lac la Biche and in 1799 made a survey of Lesser Slave Lake, the Athabasca and the Clearwater Rivers and Isle a la Crosse areas. In November 1800, he accompanied Duncan McGillivray of the North West Company, and they, with four men and an Indian guide, visited the Piegan as far south as the Highwood River then returned to the Bow River. They ascended it to where the banks rose, 'two hundred feet of black slatey rock'. The next day, McGillivray, Thompson and Dumond climbed a mountain, which was hard, and rough enough to cut their shoes. They had a fine view, and Thompson commented on the mass of even peaks. After four hours climbing, they returned to camp. The general opinion is they were in the Exshaw-Gap area and may have climbed a shoulder of Grotto Mountain. Later the same year, McGillivray and Thompson tried to cross the mountains by the Clearwater and Brazeau Rivers but the attempt was a failure.

By 1801, McGillivray was badly crippled with rheumatism and had to return to Cumberland House. Before going he told Thompson and Hughes, who was left in command, to cross the mountains. So, in June 1801, they travelled to the first and second ranges of mountains by the Saskatchewan and Sheep (or Ram) Rivers. With great difficulty, they reached a lake, but were forced to turn back. When they returned to the Saskatchewan River, they built another canoe. Hughes, the guide and one man returned to the Fort. Thompson and eight men continued up the Saskatchewan, until they reached rock walls of 300 to 500 feet, when they, too, turned back.

In 1806, Thompson was at Rocky Mountain House on the Saskatchewan River, and he sent Jack Finlay across the mountains to build canoes on the other side for a proposed trading venture. Thompson, his family, and the men reached the top of Howse Pass on June 25, 1807 (Joseph Howse, a Hudson's Bay man, used it two years later and named it). Thompson followed the Blaeberry River and reached the Columbia River (near Moberly Station on the Canadian Pacific Railway) by the end of the month. Thompson named it the Kootenay. Not until 1811 would he realize that it was the Columbia, which flows north for two hundred odd miles before turning in a big bend to flow south and finally west. He ascended the Columbia after building canoes and reached Lake Windermere, where he built Kootenae House (near Athalmere). The mountains along the Columbia he named Nelson's Mountains (Selkirk and Purcell ranges today). In the spring of 1808, he reached Columbia Lake and portaged Canal Flats to the Kootenay River. He explored the Fort Steele region, portaged Kent Falls to Kootenay Lake, traded for furs and returned overland by horse to Kootenae House.

In 1810, Thompson and his family crossed Howse Pass from the west where he killed two Wood buffalo, proving that these animals were present in the mountains. He continued east for his rotating year's leave but was stopped at Rainy Lake. His orders, according to his *Narrative*, were to go down to the mouth of the Columbia River by August 1811.

When Thompson reached Rocky Mountain House he started west by horse with William Henry, while his canoes, men and supplies went by river. En route, because the Piegan were angry at Thompson for trading guns with the Kootenay and because of a recent battle the Piegan had lost, they separated Thompson from his men. In the end, he decided to cross the mountains via the headwaters of the Athabasca, rather than by using his accustomed route over Howse Pass.

After a difficult trip through heavy and fallen timber, and a difficult time building sleds and making snowshoes, Thompson and his men ascended the Whirlpool River to the top of Athabasca Pass, reaching it January 10, 1811. He descended Wood River to the Columbia River near Canoe River, where he stopped at Boat Encampment until April. Thompson continued his journey up the Columbia, exploring to Spokane House and then to the mouth of the Snake River, Idaho. There, on July 9, 1811, he raised a pole with a flag and a paper, claiming the territory for Great Britain and the trade for the North West Company. On July 15, 1811, Thompson reached Fort Astoria, which had been constructed three months before by John Jacob Astor's Pacific Fur Company. Thompson returned up the Columbia by Arrow Lake, past Revelstoke and the Big Bend to Boat Encampment. He had travelled the entire length of the Columbia River. Then he crossed Athabasca Pass, in May, 1812, for the last time, before going east to Fort William.

After he retired, Thompson worked on his great map of Northwestern America which he delivered to the North West Company in 1813. It hung on the dining room wall in the Company's headquarters at Fort William for many years. He wrote many letters urging the British to claim the Oregon Territory, by right of exploration and of settlement. Unfortunately, the British authorities were not prepared to press hard for the Oregon Territory and in 1846 yielded to Polk's threats and accepted the 49th Parallel as the boundary between British and American territory.

Thompson died February 10, 1857, but before then he compiled the *Narrative* from his Journals. That historical work alone was a very real accomplishment. Thompson was unsuccessful in his attempt to have it published and not until 1916 did the *Narrative* become available to the public.

When he discovered Athabasca Pass, he opened up what was to become the main fur trade highway to the Pacific for many years to come. Today, Thompson is still considered one of the world's great mapmakers and surveyors. His memorials are a river in British Columbia which he did not see, a cairn on Athabasca Pass and the David Thompson Highway, which follows his old route from Rocky Mountain House to the Saskatchewan Crossing.

From the beginning the North West Company, because of its many voyageurs, penetrated far into new territory inland. The time came when costs of long distance transport and too many men became a disadvantage and the men deserted to the Hudson's Bay Company. Competition between the companies became bitter and led to amalgamation in 1821 under the Hudson's Bay Company's name. No longer could the Indian take advantage of the rivalry of the fur companies. After 1821, the Hudson's Bay Company enjoyed a monopoly of the fur trade.

In 1832, the Hudson's Bay Company tried to improve relations and trade with the Piegan so they built Piegan Post near the junction of Bow Fort Creek at the Bow River. J.E. Harriott was in charge, with Colin Fraser, Hugh Munro, Donald McDonald, and James Bird, Junior, under him. They left it after it was built in the spring of 1833 and did not return until August. The post had been partially burned, but trade continued until January 1834, when it was abandoned. It had not been a success, so Rocky Mountain House, which had been closed, was reopened. Sometime later the Sarsi burned Piegan Post. The old stone chimneys were still easily located as late as the 1920s. By the people in the west it was always called "Old Bow Fort", and became a landmark for explorers and travellers.

David Douglas, a botanist, who worked under Professor Hooker at the Glasgow Botanical Gardens, was sent by him to Canada to collect specimens. Douglas crossed Athabasca Pass in 1827 on his way east. At Norway House he met Sir John Franklin and Sir John Richardson, who were on the Second Arctic Expedition. More important he met Thomas Drummond, who was a botanist for the Expedition. Drummond had been on Athabasca Pass in October when he had picked blueberries. The two men exchanged information and specimens. Douglas returned home with the Expedition, after joining them later at York Factory.

Drummond's name is identified with several of our flowers, because the same species he found further north grow in our higher altitudes; Dryas Drummondii and Drummond's Rock Cress are among these. Douglas's name is commemorated in the Douglas Fir and Mount Douglas. However, David Douglas's fame in the Canadian Rockies results from the two mountains at Athabasca Pass which he named Mount Brown and Mount Hooker, and to which he gave fantastic elevations.

George Simpson, who began his career in the Hudson's Bay Company in 1820 had, by 1839, become Governor-in-Chief of all the Company's territories, a commercial empire which covered the North West Territories and reached to the Pacific Ocean. Simpson, though pompous and authoritarian, was a superb administrator. On his epic journeys across Canada he savoured the talents of his own Scottish piper and the favours of comely Indian girls.

In 1828, Simpson went to the headwaters of the Peace River and into New Caledonia (British Columbia). He followed the Thompson River from Kamloops Lake to the junction with the Fraser and down to the Pacific. Fort Langley had been started in 1827 to combat American coastal fur trade. He continued down the coastal waters to Fort Vancouver, near the mouth of the Columbia, built in 1824-1825 as a result of Simpson's earlier visit. This exploratory trip proved the importance of control of the Columbia, the only navigable river to the Pacific. However, the lower Columbia, south of the 49th Parallel, was to be lost to Canada by the Oregon Treaty of 1846.

In 1841, Simpson (earlier in the year he became Sir George) started on a journey around the world. He travelled across the plains at fifty miles a day, driving both his men and himself. At Frenchman's Butte on the Little Red Deer River he overtook Sinclair and his party of emigrants. Chief Factor John Rowand accompanied Simpson's party when they left Fort Edmonton on horseback, accompanied by pack horses, with the Indian, Peechee, as their guide. They met the Reverend Mr. Robert Rundle and they camped that night at Smoking Weed Camp near Wetaskiwin.

The Simpson diary from August 1-3 tells of his trip from Devil's Head to the waterfall on Cascade Mountain, which he calls the 'Spout'. There is little doubt Simpson and Rowand were the first white men to come through the pass at Devil's Head to Lake Minnewanka and into the Bow River Valley in the Banff area. Peechee led them to Devil's Lake by entering at the east end. As he said it was his home, Simpson named the lake 'Peechee', but the name was not recorded and when the name 'Minnewanka' was given to the lake, Mount Peechee in the Fairholme Range was named for the guide.

Simpson and his men ascended the Bow and crossed on a raft they built to reach the mouth of Healy Creek. They went over Simpson Pass, which was named for him, because he was the first white man to cross it. He carved his and Rowand's initials on a tree with the date of the crossing. This tree was found many years later by one of the Brewster packers, who gave it to James Brewster of Banff Simpson pushed into the Kootenay Valley, through "a horrid gorge in a mountain of red rock" (later called Sinclair Canyon) to the Columbia Valley. They penetrated the timber to the confluence of the Simpson and Vermilion Rivers (today a cairn commemorates Simpson's visit). From there, he continued to Fort Vancouver. When Peechee left him at Fort Colvile to return home, Simpson gave him his telescope. Simpson continued around the world and later wrote his book.

The Reverend Mr. Robert Rundle was born at Mylor, Cornwall, England. As a youth he was a lay preacher and was ordained in 1839. In 1840 he was sent to Norway House as a missionary, and on October 18th of that year he was sent to Fort Edmonton. He worked out of there ranging over the prairies to preach to the Blackfoot and the Stonys.

In 1844 in his diary Rundle records that he tried to climb a mountain somewhere along the Bow River, but it is not certain which mountain. In 1847, he records his visit to Lake Minnewanka and says that he put his initials on a tree "RTR July 1, 1847"; but he gave no indication of reaching Cascade Mountain or the valley of Banff. There is no mention of either the waterfall on Cascade Mountain or Bow Falls. Many years later James Hector named Rundle Mountain for the pioneer missionary, because an Indian said Rundle had been in the area; but unfortunately written records do not reveal exactly the location visited by Rundle.

The question of the right to trade in the Oregon Territory caused the Hudson's Bay Company in 1841 to send some settlers there. James Sinclair, a most interesting man of varied experience, was chosen to lead this group to their new home. They met on the plain near Fort Garry and were mainly Metis from the Red River Settlement. They, with their families, hoped to better their lot in new country.

Sinclair took his group from Fort Garry to Forts Ellice, Carleton, Pitt and Edmonton. At Fort Edmonton, he found instructions from George Simpson to go over Athabasca Pass to Fort Vancouver. Sinclair was disappointed at missing both Simpson and Rowand, who had left a few weeks earlier, and decided to try a new pass. A Cree guide, Broken Arm, told him there were three passes, that no white man had seen, and he would take him over one of them.

The party left Fort Edmonton the second week in August, 1841, going south and southwest to La Biche River (Little Red Deer) and following an Assiniboine (Stony) trail through the foothills and through Devil's Gap to Devil's Lake. Simpson had travelled on the northwest side of the lake, but Broken Arm took Sinclair along the southeast side. Then they passed through a steep gorge (probably Carrot Creek) to the Bow Valley. They crossed the Bow River at Canmore and went along by the Three Sisters up a branch of the Spray River to White Man Pass, between three mountains (now Mounts Warre, Vavasour and Currie) and followed a stream or river (Cross) down into Kootenay River Valley. Then they followed Simpson's route to Fort Vancouver. The journey took five months.

In late 1850, Sinclair took a small party of Company men over his 1841 route to Fort Colvile, when he went on business for Simpson, Again in mid-August 1854, Sinclair started on his last trip. He had his family and father-in-law with him as well as his party. That was the worst trip for they crossed Kananaskis Pass. They abandoned the carts at the south of the Kananaskis River, after using parts of them to build saddles (remains of the carts were found in 1859 by Blakiston). Their Cree guide got lost and it is assumed they went by the upper (south) Kananaskis Pass, because they had to travel on foot, and suffered great hardship. They had snow three feet deep to cope with and had to kill some of the oxen for food. However, they followed a creek down to a river (Palliser) and reached Kootenay Valley. They arrived at Fort Walla Walla December 16, 1854 after nearly seven months. Sinclair left his family and took the rest of the party to Fort Vancouver. He became Master of Fort Walla Walla for the Hudson's Bay Company, and was eventually killed in the Indian wars near The Cascades on the Columbia River in 1856.

Because of the increasing problem of the Oregon Territory, England sent Lieut. H.J. Warre, aide de camp to commander of forces in Canada,

the Reverend Mr. Robert Terrill Rundle

and Lieut. M. Vavasour, R.E., on a secret military mission to report on the practicability of establishing military posts on the lower Columbia River and of transporting troops to the area.

On May 5, 1845, they left Montreal with Sir George Simpson and party for the Red River and Fort Garry. They were then sent with Peter Skene Ogden as guide and a dozen voyageurs. After reaching the Bow River, they ascended it and crossed a pass in about 50°30' N. Lat. (White Man) and reached Fort Vancouver near the end of the summer. During the winter they explored American settlements on the Williamette River, the mouth of the Columbia and Puget Sound. Christmas was spent at Fort Victoria.

They started on the return journey March 25, 1846, going to the Rapids of Death and to Walla Walla and then by horses to Fort Colvile. They followed the Columbia River to Boat Encampment and then crossed Athabasca Pass. They were out of provisions so Warre and two men set out for Jasper House.

Fortunately they met Father De Smet and party in ten miles and were able to procure the sleds, dogs and provisions sent by the Hudson's Bay Company. From here the two officers used the well-travelled route to the east and ultimately reached England. Two mountains at White Man Pass are named for Warre and Vavasour.

Belgian-born Father Pierre Jean De Smet emigrated to America, and entering the Jesuit Order, was ordained in 1827. He was sent to the Oregon Territory in 1840, and established a mission for the Flatheads in 1841.

In the fall of 1845, he went on a mission to the Blackfoot, setting out from Fort Vancouver in Oregon. He ascended the Columbia, visited the hot springs (probably Radium), and left the valley by Sinclair Canyon. Then he followed the Kootenay to another river (Cross River) and reached a pass (White Man) and there, where the waters divide, he raised a cross. He journeyed along the Spray and mentioned Pyramid Peaks in the mountains (perhaps one was Mount Assiniboine). After following Goat Range through burnt timber, which he called 'vexatious', he finally reached the Bow River. He met Stonys near the Gap and that night they camped close to one another. In the morning Father De Smet found the dogs had eaten his cassock collar, his shoes, and one leg of his leather britches. He travelled to Rocky Mountain House where he met Rundle, who mentions it in his diary, then to Fort Edmonton. Both missionaries spent the winter there.

March 12, Father De Smet left for home. As he was told the pass would be difficult and snowshoes were new to him, Father De Smet fasted to reduce his weight before he made the journey. The good-natured priest had many a fall before he mastered the snowshoes, much to the amusement of his companions. He went to Jasper House and he baptized thirty Iroquois at Roche De Smet which he called 'Sugar Loaf Mountain'. West of Jasper House his party encountered Warre and Vavasour, whom he had met previously at

Lake Kalispell. Father De Smet crossed Athabasca Pass on snowshoes and followed Wood River to Boat Encampment on the Columbia. There he found the cache of flour, ham, deer and sugar left for him by the Hudson's Bay men. He followed the Columbia to Fort Vancouver, reaching it by midsummer.

All of these explorers and missionaries wrote of the mountains, the rivers, the wild animals, fowl and fish, and the climate, which was an important factor in their work, winter or summer. Without the bounties of nature they would have suffered greater hardships than they did.

In 1838, a renewal for twenty-one years of the Hudson's Bay Company's right to trade from the Great Lakes west to the Pacific had been granted by the British government, but the end of monopoly rule by the Company was in sight. Canada was becoming aware of the land to the west. Canadian statesmen were beginning to think of a larger British North America from the Atlantic to the Pacific and from the 49th Parallel to the Arctic. Also they were aware of the western push in the United States, and felt that Canada needed to consider settlement on the prairies to be assured of keeping them within her boundaries.

By 1857, an inquiry into the affairs of the Hudson's Bay Company by a Parliamentary committee in London led to the recommendation that the part of the country suitable for settlement be annexed, and all the rest would remain for the fur trade. At the same time the Secretary of State for the Colonies authorized an expedition to explore the southern part of the Hudson's Bay Company land. This expedition, headed by Captain John Palliser, ended the period of exploration by the fur traders in the west.

VI

New Light
on the Rockies

Thompson and McGillivray had touched the outer border of the Rockies when they came up the Bow River. The Hudson's Bay Company had tried to establish Old Bow Fort, almost beside the mountains. Sir George Simpson dashed through the Bow River Valley, and the Reverend Mr. Robert Rundle climbed a portion of a mountain somewhere in the neighbourhood. To these men, Rundle excepted, the mountains were only a barrier to the fur trade and were bordered by hostile Indian country. With the Palliser Expedition of 1857, sponsored by the British government, a new era was to begin in this long neglected area of the land.

The Expedition was to have a scientific, geographic and political character. Captain Palliser, as the leader, applied his organizing ability and intelligence to his work, but had only an observer's interest in the future of the west. He reported unfavourably to the government on the possibilities of agriculture and settlement on the southern prairies, and said there was no good railway route in all British territory through the mountains to the Pacific. However, in spite of the fact twenty years passed before more exploration was undertaken, we cannot blame him altogether. He came in a dry period; others who came later in wet periods found it a good land. No one at that time could foresee the settlement or exodus of the future that would prove both opinions right.

Dr. James Hector, M.D. was chosen as naturalist-geologist for the Expedition by the Royal Geographical Society. He was methodical and conscientious in his work. He made maps, listed minerals, recorded climate, and kept a record of fossils and plants. He explored an amazing amount of country and his interest in the Indians was real, leading him to compile vocabularies of the different tribes. After Bourgeau left, Hector collected the botanical specimens. Above all, Hector had a sense of humour, was cheerful and kind to white and Indian alike.

Eugene Bourgeau, the botanist and an affable companion, was indefatigable in his work, and collected some 819 species. He had 10,000 specimens of dried plants and seeds which were sent to Kew Gardens in England. Of these, fifty varieties were Alpine flora collected at 8,400 feet. Unfortunately, he was here for a limited time only, having promised to do research in the Caucasian Mountains the following year. Bourgeau Range in Banff is his memorial.

Lieutenant Thomas W. Blakiston, R.A. joined the Expedition as a magnetic observer. He was difficult to get along with, being both overbearing and sarcastic.

John W. Sullivan was to be an astronomer as well as a secretary to Palliser. He had mathematical ability and some French, and he and Bourgeau became friends. His relations with Blakiston, however, deteriorated. Sullivan made his own astronomical observations, looked after accounts and helped the others where he could.

Hector explored the country around the Thickwood Hills in the fall of 1857, and in the winter went to Lac Ste. Anne to get horses for the next spring. When he arrived, he found the Metis were away hunting, so he made a trip to Rocky Mountain House, explored the country and made friends with the Indians. He later followed the Saskatchewan, nearly to Fort Pitt, to map the river.

In the spring of 1858, Palliser sent Blakiston up the North Saskatchewan River to make magnetic observations, while the rest of the party went to Eagle Hills. Blakiston rejoined them south of the forks of the Medicine and Red Deer Rivers, then he explored the North and South Kootenay Pass area. Palliser and Sullivan explored south along the mountains to a place where they could see Chief Mountain, near Waterton. Then they returned to the Bow River and followed it north to meet the rest of the party at Old Bow Fort.

Hector and Bourgeau went up the Bow together but Hector left Bourgeau at Cascade Mountain. Hector went west through the Bow Valley and continued up the Bow until he turned west and crossed Vermilion Pass to the upper Kootenay River. He followed it to its source, crossed a height of land and, turning north, followed the Beaverfoot River to the Kicking Horse River. Where he turned east on this river he was kicked severely in the chest while trying to help his horse cross the river. He was unconscious for so long the men decided he was dead and were ready to bury him. After he regained consciousness, they named the river 'Kicking Horse'. Though suffering greatly, Hector managed to get his men over the pass. Not having found any game on the west slope of the mountains, they were starving. Nimrod, his guide, fortunately shot a moose when they arrived at the Bow River, a stream which the Indian recognized. Hector followed the Bow to its source, crossed Bow Pass, and followed the Mistaya (Grizzly) River (also known as the South or Little Fork of the Saskatchewan, or Bear Creek) to the North Saskatchewan River. He followed it, examined the valley of the Big Horn River and went to Fort Edmonton by the Wolfe's Track and the west Blackfoot Trail. There were three Blackfoot trails going north and south: the west, the middle and the east.

Palliser, having been delayed, finally left Old Bow Fort, followed the Bow River to the mouth of the Kananaskis River, then followed it over the pass (North Kananaskis Pass, because he rode) and down Palliser River to the Kootenay River. He recrossed by north Kootenay Pass and used the middle Blackfoot Trail to Fort Edmonton. The three parties were all there by October. Blakiston left the Expedition and went down the Saskatchewan and the fur brigade, leaving the others to winter at Fort Edmonton. Here, Captain Arthur Brisco and William R. Mitchell, who had been travelling and hunting together, joined Palliser as an independent party.

Palliser spent part of the winter of 1858-59 at Rocky Mountain House, making friends with the Blackfoot, taking astronomical observations, and attending to maps, finances and accounts. He also explored the territory south of Fort Edmonton. Hector made several trips that winter. The November-December one is of interest to us because he followed the Little Red Deer River to Waiparous Creek and, thence, to the Ghost River, which he hoped to go up, but the ice was not solid. He managed to go on foot to the base of the mountains near Devil's Head, then returned to Fort Edmonton by Rocky Mountain House in time for Christmas. On another trip he went to Fort Assiniboine, on the Athabasca River; to Jasper House; and finally to the Whirlpool River. He wanted to go up to Athabasca Pass but his guide had injured his leg. Hector climbed to a high point to try to identify Mount Hooker and Mount Brown, the fabulous peaks of David Douglas's report. Then Hector made his way back to Fort Edmonton.

In the spring Hector and his guide, Peter Erasmus, had to wait for James Beads, whom they hoped would get back from the East with dispatches saying the Expedition could return to England via the Pacific Ocean. Meanwhile Palliser took the eastern Blackfoot Trail to the Hand Hills where Hector, Beads and Erasmus caught up with him. Then the area of southeastern Alberta was explored.

Following this exploration, Palliser and Sullivan went to North Kootenay Pass and, thence, to the Columbia River. Sullivan left the party at Bonner's Ferry to go to Fort Colvile by the regular route and Palliser travelled by canoe down Kootenay Lake and River to the Columbia River and on to Fort Colvile. Sullivan explored to Moyie Lake, while Palliser went as far as the Kettle River on the boundary, still looking for a good all-British route to the Pacific.

Hector left the Cypress Hills, went west to the Bow River and up it as far as the Elbow River, which he followed upstream some distance before

Sir James Hector (seated) with Edward Whymper in 1903.

he turned north to the Bow. He was anxious to find another pass, so he turned and went north by the Pipestone and Siffleur Rivers to the North Saskatchewan. He turned west and rediscovered Howse Pass, forgotten since David Thompson's time. Hector crossed the pass and followed the Blaeberry River to the Columbia. He tried to go north, but there was too much fallen timber, so he was forced to go up the Columbia to the Kootenay past Canal Flats. He could not find a guide to take him to Moyie Lake via the Fort Steele region, so he resigned himself to going to Fort Colvile where he met the others. After financial and transportation difficulties, they all reached the Pacific and sailed for home.

In 1903, Mrs. Charles Schaffer (later Mrs. William Warren of Banff) was sitting in the small rotunda of Glacier House, when it was only an inn to feed the people from the trains. She was sketching when she heard, "I mean to see my grave", then a thump on the office counter. When Mary Schaffer went toward the desk she saw the hostess listening to an undersized, emphatic man, rather stout, who looked about seventy years old. The hostess introduced Mary to him, and she was astounded to meet the famous Dr. Hector of the Palliser Expedition. Naturally she asked him where he meant to look at his grave and Sir James told her about his trip across Vermilion Pass and the Kicking Horse River. "I completely forgot about the limber heels of my pony, so eager was I to get over with the rest of the party. The pony refused the wild stream and I gave him quite a good blow on the rump. That was the last I knew until I woke in time to behold a grave yawning for me. My friends had decided I was dead and they were doing the respectful act – putting me under the sod. This I sternly refused and having recovered my wind was ready to go off again up that wild stream. My men called the stream the Kicking Horse and do you know, I am fully convinced I could locate that grave of mine." Alas he was not to see that grave.

In the afternoon Sir James was with his son, Douglas, who had become ill. Later James called in Dr. Schaffer who diagnosed appendicitis and advised immediate removal to hospital in Revelstoke. This was not done until the next morning and in the afternoon a telegram came to Dr. Schaffer, "Twenty-four hours too late. We could not save him."

Edward Whymper, a noted English mountain climber, arrived in Glacier that night; he and the Schaffers went to Revelstoke by freight, through the courtesy of the western division superintendent, so they could be with Sir James. The freight left at 5 a.m. and should have reached Revelstoke at 9 a.m. but it did not get there until 2:50 p.m. They were just in time to join the small procession to the grave. Fortunately, an old friend of Sir James had arrived from the Klondike so he had been with Sir James.

Later in the afternoon they were all together on the lawn of the Revelstoke hotel and Sir James was delighted to meet, for the first time, Mr. Whymper with whom he had frequently corresponded. Sir James said to

Mary, "Did you hear of a place called the Great Divide? I know I could find it. It was the highest point of land we reached after our tremendous struggle up the Kicking Horse. We had been very much out of food and on reaching this place we divided a grouse among our party and one said, "We can call this the Great Divide." Mary asked if she might photograph Sir James and Mr. Whymper together and they complied. Hector gave up all further travelling, and left on the next train to return to New Zealand on the same boat by which he had so joyously come. He was destined never to return to Canada.[1] In a letter in 1928 to Dr. R.F. Zillmer of Milwaukee, Wis., Mrs. Warren wrote that Dr. Schaffer had started the monument to Sir James Hector at the Great Divide, and that he saw a photograph of it before he died.

In 1859, the Hudson's Bay Company's licence came up for renewal. The Imperial Government refused to renew it for New Caledonia, which became a crown colony named 'British Columbia'. They gave the Company a monopoly to trade east of the Rocky Mountains for twenty one years. People interested in the future of the country objected, declaring this was detrimental to settlement. No further developments took place before Confederation, but in 1870 Rupert's Land became part of the new Dominion.

In 1859, James Carnegie, the Earl of Southesk, came to Canada to travel and to hunt. He was at the age when young men took the Grand Tour in Europe, but because of the unsettled conditions there, he took his in the Canadian west.

Southesk followed the fur trade route to Fort Edmonton, then went west to the McLeod River. He followed the valley of the Medicine Tent River, and crossed a pass. From there he followed the North River (Brazeau), and came to the North Saskatchewan. At Kootenay Plain he crossed the North Saskatchewan River, where he passed a tree on which was written 'Exploratory Expedition, Aug. 23, 1859 Dr. Hector'. The inscription was just a month old. Southesk followed the Pipestone River, and reached the Bow Valley. He camped near Castle Mountain, and at Johnston Creek met a party of Stonys from whom he was able to buy much needed sheep and moose meat. He continued along the Sawback Range, passed Vermilion Lakes, and forded Forty Mile Creek. He camped at the base of Cascade Mountain, and then went on to the Old Bow Fort. From there he followed along the mountains back to Fort Edmonton, then home to England.

The Earl of Southesk was the first real tourist to come to Banff Some would argue, no doubt, that Sir George Simpson was the first, when he made his trip around the world. Simpson was a fur trader, however, looking for possible trade routes while the Earl was on a pleasure trip. This young man took a great interest in the different wild game, and carefully wrote of the

---

[1]For this story I have kept much of Mary Schaffer Warren's own wording as she wrote it for the *Calgary Herald* Supplement some time in the 1920s.

varieties of meat he ate. He carried a volume of Shakespeare's plays, and read one every evening before sleeping, while his men sat around the campfire. His comments on Shakespeare, written in the wilds of the Rocky Mountains, are both entertaining and unique. Eccentric he might have been, but he proved to his guide and men that he was boss of the trip, and though they might not like the hard mountain travel, he was going to explore the Rocky Mountains. Southesk climbed a mountain, named two for friends, hunted, and enjoyed the scenery and all kinds of wild life. Eventually his book *Saskatchewan and The Rocky Mountains*, complete with map, was published. His trophies from the trip are still preserved at Kinnaird Castle, Brechin, Angus, where he died in 1905. He is remembered by Mount Southesk, Southesk River, Southesk Pass and a cairn.

VII

The Coming of the Rails

During the period of the fur trade the Indian had lost his old way of life. He had contributed to the success of the traders and to the explorers of that period with his pemmican, his furs and his knowledge of the country. The Indians were the guides, and Indian names are used to this day for rivers, mountains, towns and cities. After 1869, however, the Indian no longer was governed by the Company. He was left to the mercy of the American whisky trader, who came to the plains from the south. The Canadian Government appeared to feel little concern for him. Until the North West Mounted Police came west in 1874, it was a bad time for the Indians.

The Gold Rush of the late 1850s in British Columbia turned men's eye's westward. In 1867, the United States bought Alaska from Russia, and Canadians began to wonder about the future of the west. Palliser had reported there were passes through the mountains. The Canadian Government, therefore sponsored expeditions led by Henry Youle Hind and S.J. Dawson which recommended that communication be opened between Canada and Red River utilizing water transportation on the Great Lakes and on the lakes and rivers west of Lake Superior, linking them by roads where necessary. Farther west Hind suggested diverting the waters of the south branch of the Saskatchewan into the Qu'Appelle River (a tributary of the Red River) to provide a continuous waterway as far as the Rockies.

The incorporation of Rupert's Land into the Canadian Union in 1870 raised the question of a transcontinental railway. This matter became particularly urgent when British Columbia joined Confederation in 1871. Surveys for the route were authorized by Sir John A. Macdonald. Walter Moberly of British Columbia had already taken steps in this direction as early as 1865 when he was surveyor-general for British Columbia. He went to Shuswap Lake, and then discovered what he named 'Eagle Pass' over the Gold Range. He continued by the Columbia River to near Revelstoke, and explored a river (Illecilliwaet) to the forks and up the north fork. This proved impassible, and as it was very late in the season and his Indians were getting restless, he did nothing about the south fork; however, he promised himself he would come back, for he believed there must be a pass over the Selkirk Range at that point. He put this in his report, but his work directed him elsewhere, so he was unable to put his theory to the test.

Joseph Trutch, the first Lieutenant-Governor of British Columbia, told Sir John A. Macdonald that Moberly was the man who knew about the mountains, so Moberly was asked to go to Ottawa. Moberly advised that a trans-mountain route should follow the Howse Pass, thence around the Big Bend, then over Eagle Pass to Shuswap Lake, and, finally, down the Thompson and Fraser Rivers to Burrard Inlet.

Sandford Fleming was appointed by the government as Engineer-in-Chief of the projected railroad, and he ordered a survey, organized in twenty-one divisions, with crews numbering about 800 men. He appointed Roderick McLennan to work with Moberly. Moberly found another practicable route by the North Thompson River to Albreda Lake and to the Yellowhead. Both men found heavy forest, fallen timber and plenty of Devil's Club (a most vicious plant with thorns that tear men's flesh through their clothes), all over the Selkirks. Moberly, who went over Eagle Pass and high up on the Selkirks by snowshoe in December, realized snow and avalanches on the Selkirks would be a problem. In 1872, he heard from Fleming that the Yellowhead Pass would be adopted.

We are not concerned here with the troubles which attended the first efforts to organize and finance the Pacific railway. It is sufficient to note that in 1881 the Federal Government finally chartered the 'Canadian Pacific Railway Company', with George Stephen, President; Duncan McIntyre, Vice-President; R.B. Angus and James J. Hill on the executive committee. Hill, a former Canadian, and a resident of St. Paul, Minn., had worked on railways in the United States and was interested in feeder-lines to American railways.

The contract with the government permitted the Company to import necessary machinery duty free, and it received 25 million acres of usable land, 25 million dollars and the guarantee that for twenty years no line would be permitted to run south of theirs except to the southwest.

In 1881, only 150 miles of track were laid, so William Cornelius Van Horne (later Sir William) was brought in from the United States to manage construction and speed it up. He promised to lay 500 miles of track in 1882, and almost succeeded. He told the company that immigration alone would not pay for the road, but that they needed their own pullmans, diners, telegraph and express. Thomas G. Shaughnessy (later Baron Shaughnessy) came a month later to work with him.

In April 1882, a Bill was passed by Parliament authorizing the use of the pass that was most direct, south of the Yellowhead. This meant Kicking Horse Pass. How the railroad was to get over the Selkirks was still unknown.

Late in 1881, James J. Hill recommended that Major A.B. Rogers, an American civil engineer, be appointed to survey a practicable route through the Canadian Rockies. Rogers left at once for Kamloops. In April 1881 he and his nephew, Albert Rogers, and Indian guides left for the Selkirks. Rogers had read Moberly's report, and had been advised by Moberly to try the south fork of the Illecilliwaet River for a pass.

They had a terrible trip, plagued by cold, snow and insufficient supplies. Finally Rogers was compelled to return. He determined to try it from the east side of the Selkirks. The next year he got horses and packhorses, and with his nephew set out from Spokane. He left Albert at Wild Horse mining camp (later Fort Steele) to take the pack train to the mouth of the Kicking Horse and up it to the Great Divide. This was a very difficult route, and really not fit for horses.

Rogers, meantime, followed the Columbia, crossed Brisco Range to the Cross River and came to the Bow Valley over White Man Pass. He reached the railroad camp at the Gap on July 15th. The next day they moved on, leaving Frederick Aylmer (later the Honourable Frederick Aylmer) to go over Kananaskis Pass. In three days they were opposite Healy Creek and Donald McMillan left to cross Simpson Pass, to explore its possibilities. The main party moved up the Bow, reaching the flat where Lake Louise station now is and camped. Rogers went the next day to the junction of the Bow and Bath Creek, named for Rogers' unscheduled bath, after he fell off his horse in attempting to cross the creek in flood. Charles Sproat left to go to Bow Summit to explore the route. The following day Rogers reached the east end of Kicking Horse Lake (Wapta), where they were to meet Albert. When he did not arrive Rogers sent men out to search in likely directions. Tom Wilson, who had become Rogers' guide, and Fred Palling went down the south side of the Kicking Horse. They met Albert in a state of starvation and exhaustion. He had left the pack-horses at the mouth of the Kicking Horse with one Indian, and continued on foot upstream with the other Indian, whom he sent up the Ottertail Valley, on the chance he, Albert, had taken the wrong trail.

Rogers was indefatigable and visited all the camps to make certain the other passes were not more direct. He instructed Albert to run a line down the Kicking Horse. Finally Rogers reached Beaver Creek and following it upstream discovered the famous pass which bears his name. Rogers returned to wire the Company that the pass over the Selkirks had been found. It was August 1882.

That same year James Ross, engineer for the Rocky Mountains Division, sent Charles Aeneas Shaw to check Rogers' survey for the railway. Rogers had reported it would be necessary to put a tunnel through a mountain to continue up the Bow Valley. Shaw found a valley near the one running from Devil's Lake, so he followed this new valley around the north end of Tunnel Mountain into Bow Valley. This route eliminated the tunnel, but the mountain has been called 'Tunnel' Mountain ever since.

The Canadian Government wished confirmation of Rogers' discovery, so they cabled Sandford Fleming, who was living in England, to come to Canada and go over Rogers Pass. He reached Calgary August 24, 1881. Fleming's son and the Reverend George M. Grant, who had accompanied Fleming when he went through Yellowhead Pass in 1872, were with him.

After coming to Calgary by rail, they rode to the Kicking Horse Pass, where they finally caught up with Rogers. He assured Fleming there really was a pass through the Selkirks. The Fleming party struggled up to the summit on foot. It was a beautiful place, with Syndicate Peak (later Mount Sir Donald) towering above. They toasted the discovery with brook water and founded the Alpine Club of Canada. They feasted on blueberries and raspberries, smoked cigars, then played leapfrog. Fleming's party continued on foot through the Box Canyon (Albert Canyon) to Eagle Pass. Fleming, his son, and Grant reached Kamloops twenty-three days after leaving Calgary. Fleming sent a wire to the government that all was well.

On October 16, 1883, Sandford Fleming wrote a confidential letter to Sir Charles Tupper, High Commissioner for Canada in England, giving some details and recording for us some of the emotion he must have felt:

... It is the first through trip of any kind on the line of railroad now in process of construction. It is the first through trip over the Selkirks. Major Rogers has never been through and through. I doubt if any Indian has.... The time in the mountains was about four weeks, about two of which we had no horses... we were compensated by the satisfaction in beholding the magnificent mountain scenery near the source of the Bow river, the Kicking Horse, the Selkirks and the Columbian Ranges with their huge glaciers, some of them miles in extent...

In August 1885, the Marquis of Lansdowne, Governor-General of Canada, had travelled to within twenty-five miles of the railhead at Rogers Pass, and had expected to be at the driving of the last spike on November 7th. He had ordered a silver spike mounted on a plaque for the event; however, Van Horne had no faith in gold or silver spikes, and said only people who had been connected with the railroad were to be present.

The last spike ceremony took place in Eagle Pass, where the east and west lines of construction met at a place named 'Craigellachie'. Major Rogers held the tie in position, while Donald A. Smith, a major shareholder in the Company, drove the spike amid silence, each man thinking his own thoughts; then a spontaneous cheer rang out. No bands playing, no telegraph wires singing – just a job well done, at great cost in money, lives and hardship.

The first through passenger train left Montreal June 28, 1886, and the first through freight, of twenty cars, July 6, 1886.

At a later date when Lady Macdonald, the wife of Sir John A.

Macdonald, was travelling from Donald Station to Banff, Superintendent Niblock of the Canadian Pacific Railway western division was escorting her in his private car, *Earnscliffe*. He wired, "Have bouquet of flowers for car *Earnscliffe* on arrival number 2." The agent wondered at the nature of the request; however, when Lady Macdonald arrived she was presented in a dignified and proper manner with a bag of flour. When the wire was checked it was found that somehow it had been changed to read 'Have bag of flour'. Such were the trials of early superintendents of the railway.

VIII

The Old
and the New

The Canadian Pacific Railway was the first real wedge into an area that hitherto had been virtually unknown. To the fur traders the Rockies had been a barrier, and the Indians on the adjacent plains had become hostile as evidenced by Palliser's trouble with the Blackfoot.

However, the area was well known by the Stony, Cree and Kootenay Indians hunting, trading or fighting with one another. Several old Indian trails are known to the author. One followed the south side of the Bow River to the Spray River which the Indians forded above Spray bridge. The trail followed the ridge to the site of the Banff Springs Hotel, then to the place where the Administration Building is located. It continued to the Cave and Basin and on to Healy Creek; finally it ascended Simpson Pass and descended the watershed to the other side of the Rockies.

A branch-trail turned off at the Spray and followed a route along the foot of Mt. Rundle, branched to White Man Pass and the Sinclair Trail. Another trail followed up the north side of the Bow River, to a point where Pete Young later had a garden at Anthracite, crossed the Cascade River and went across the flats behind Tunnel Mountain and over the south end of it to just west of the spot where Muskrat Street comes to a dead end today, to connect with the south side trail going west. Farther west another ford from the trail on the north side also met the southside trail at the mouth of Healy Creek. This almost forgotten information on the trails was obtained from David McDougall at Morley, who had come to the Hot Springs with the Indians in the very early 1870s. Andrew Sibbald told me about Pete Young and another man who had come from Montana by covered wagon and ox-team in the late seventies; they traded their outfit to McDougall for horses to follow the north side trail of the Bow into the mountains.[1]

---

[1]Will Fear confirmed this information in a letter to N.K. Luxton. A copy of the letter is in the Archives of the Canadian Rockies, Banff, Alberta.

Of course, Sir George Simpson's visit to the area in 1841 is the first recorded one. Peechee, his Cree guide who lived on the shore of Devil's Lake, obviously took him over the old Indian trail. Close on Simpson's heels came Sinclair, using both White Man Pass and Kananaskis Pass. The missionary Robert Rundle came next in 1847. Then came Sir James Hector in 1858 and 1859 and Nimrod his guide who conducted him over the old trails, taking him to Bow Falls where Hector noticed the strange formation of Rundle and Tunnel Mountains. Hector named many of the mountains: Cascade, Rundle, Terrace (from the strata, later renamed Sulphur), Sawback, Castle, and Ball as well as the Pipestone Pass and River. Bourgeau on the same expedition named Grotto and Wind (Lougheed) Mountains. Palliser named the Fairholme Range and Brazeau Mountain. Thus we see the white man leaving his marks very early, all recorded on the map accompanying Palliser's Report, the first reliable map for the area.

The Earl of Southesk followed in 1859-1860, then came a period of little known penetration which lasted until the seventies. David McDougall, a trader, travelled with Indians up the Kananaskis and over the pass; also to Devil's Lake by the Dry Fork of the Ghost; and to the Middle Springs and the Cave and Basin by the south trail on various trips in the early seventies. The Indians brought their sick to the Springs and they told him it was a 'peace grounds' where they traded safely with their enemies, the Kootenay. They also showed him where they had Sun Dances on Bow Flats, the present day location of the Banff Springs golf course.

As word of the gold strike along the Fraser became known, some prospectors came to this area to prospect or in the hope of reaching British Columbia. William Pearce tells us there was an old log cabin on the sand bank on the south side of the Bow, about 150 yards west of the bridge, which was obviously a prospector's hut; but who built it was never discovered. In 1887, Pete Young said he had built a log shack on Sulphur Mountain, in the late seventies, on the terrace above Cave and Birch Avenues. He added that he was not interested in the Springs because he had seen the Indians wash in them! There are no records, oral or otherwise, other than these scattered notes, of white men in this area prior to the railway.

When the Canadian Government decided to build a railway, survey crews were sent to map prospective routes. Through the 1880s and into the early 1900s the area of the National Parks was surveyed. G.M. Dawson included a map in his Geological Survey of 1882 to 1885. These early survey reports were geological and natural history surveys as well, reporting on minerals, coal, rocks, forests and wild life. Thus we learn that the country of the Bow River and its tributaries had been devastated by many forest fires, probably started from natural causes.

Survey methods and instruments had improved greatly by 1866. From then on topographical, and later, triangulation surveys were made.

First government tent-office at Siding 29.

The country was photographed by survey crews, utilizing the new science of photogrammetry. The work of those early Dominion Land Surveyors was not easy. They were out in all kinds of weather, from below freezing to extreme heat. They penetrated thick forests or struggled through fallen timber and burnt areas. They climbed many unnamed peaks, establishing sites for other crews to follow, and their often delicate equipment had to be taken up as well. They were in unknown country far from any supply base, and all too frequently were exhausted and starved before they reached a base camp. Building a stone base to hold their survey markers on a snow-covered peak was exhausting and cold work – even to find the rocks was difficult. The marker had to be set firmly enough to withstand gales on a mountain top.

These men were our first mountaineers, but few peaks bear their names. Too many to list here, surveyors are often forgotten in the history of the opening of this area. They paved the way for later mountaineers and for the roads which would follow valleys or passes which they had gone through in earlier years.

By 1881, The Canadian Pacific Railway surveyors were in the mountains, and by 1883, Siding 29 was established on the railway. This was in the area, to the north and south of the tracks, east of the Buffalo Paddock toward Mount Cascade waterfall. The Canadian Pacific Railway built a section house next to the log station on the south side of the tracks, just east of today's highway.

The railway brought with it, besides the regular crews, the usual quota of drifters, prospectors and traders. The labourers for the railway got out timber for ties and cordwood. The area had been exploited ever since man came, first by the Indians for furs, particularly beaver, and now the white man had come to carry on new forms of exploitation. Various timber permits were taken out first. By 1883, coal was found at Anthracite, the first station east of Siding 29. The discovery of coal, of course, led to further industry.

The coal at Anthracite, where the seam was at ground level because of the mountain formation, was first mined for local use only. Then the Canadian Anthracite Coal Company took it over in 1885. There was a demand for coal in the east, though the chief market was for the Canadian Pacific Railway locomotives. The depression in the nineties had its effect, but the Company had other difficulties as well. The semi-anthracite coal was very friable (easily crumbled), the seam was steepening rapidly, and there was little working space on the north east side of the railroad. McNeil, who owned the company, closed it in 1897 so he could concentrate on the Canmore mine which had been discovered in 1886. Anthracite became a ghost town, as the miners left for Canmore, and other residents moved to Banff.

In 1881, Joe Healy (or Heely) had traded with an Indian for a piece of ore which he took to Fort Benton, Mont. to be appraised. It was fairly high in silver content, so Healy came back to do some prospecting around Castle Mountain (Eisenhower) in 1882.

In the meantime, Joe Smith, who had worked on the railway construction from Winnipeg to Calgary, had decided, in 1883, to settle at Castle Mountain. He intended to trap for furs. Word of Healy's ore had gone around, and prospectors started to come in 1883. By the time the railway reached Castle in 1884, Silver City, as the settlement that sprang up was called, was booming.

When A.P. Coleman came to survey in the Selkirks, he stopped at Morley to see his brother. David McDougall asked him if he would stop at Silver City to look at a claim McDougall had staked there. Coleman examined around the large cirque, and reported there was no silver, only some copper, zinc, galena and iron ore in the area. While in Silver City, Coleman stayed at The Miner's Home, a hotel run by Minnie McDougall and her brother, Moses.

Another hotel was run by Grew and Patterson. Joe Smith had built a rooming house and pool hall. There were several saloons and another pool hall, as well as log houses and tents where the miners lived. Two North West Mounted Police were stationed at the site to keep order. Dr. Sweet set up an office. About 285 to 300 men, seven married women and five girls were working in Silver City. The floating prospectors may have numbered one hundred or so. Father Lacombe came through at one time, and held a service in Joe Smith's pool hall.

The *Heatherington Mine*, the *Queen of the Hills*, the *Home Stake* and the *Alberta* were company claims, worked day and night. A couple of them even had night guards.

The end came in 1885, and Silver City, though its residents at one time considered having it surveyed and registered as 'Silverton', became a ghost town, almost overnight. In 1888, when William Spotswood Green, an English minister, went to see Joe Smith, he wrote, "The empty log houses were empty shells, the streets were grass grown and the station had little other than the water tower to supply the locomotives. Two section men and their wives had a house they used, but of the prospectors and miners there were no signs." The Reverend Green missed Joe, who was away trapping.

Smith sold watches, shoelaces and buttons to the navvies, as a side line, until the railroad was finished, but his main interests were trapping and reading. Though his pool hall and rooming house were moved away for the lumber, he lived on in a small house. During 1914 to 1918 he had neighbours, when the government established an Internment Camp for registered aliens at Castle (Silver City), as the station was named. Later, a movie company rebuilt "Silver City" to make the movie, "The Alaskan". Joe, then an old man, relived for a short time life as it used to be in the old town.

I remember well Joe Smith's recollections of life in Silver City. He had many friends in Banff, who visited him to talk of earlier days. It was their concern for him, when he became blind, that brought about his move, in 1937, to the Lacombe Home, south of Calgary, where he died shortly after.

Joe Smith at Silver City.

In the meantime, Siding 29 had grown also. Some stores had been erected on the north side of the tracks toward Cascade Mountain. Ferland and Company of Calgary had a general store; L.C. Fulmer had a lumber yard and store; Fred Woodworth handled the mail out of Fulmer's; Carlin, Lake and French had a general store along the highway south of the tracks, Dunn and Lineham of Calgary had a butcher shop; Tom Winnett ran a furniture store; Pat Quinlan ran the Billiard Saloon; and then came the Alpine Motel. These were all log buildings, put up hastily, and placed along the railroad or the road leading from the station. E. and J. Rauch had a stable on the north side of the railroad tracks where they kept work teams, and Billy Barker handled freight and express for their business. There was a still, near the foot of the falls on Cascade Mountain, where bootleg-whisky was made. Dave Keefe and his brother had a hotel which they called 'Banff Hotel' after Siding 29 was renamed.

From all this, one will realize it was frontier country and settlement was of a typical frontier type. Demand for lumber and coal, hopes of quick wealth, and the everyday needs of the miners at Anthracite, about eight miles to the east, and of the people living at Siding 29, led to the usual exploitation of the natural resources.

In 1883, Van Horne, returning from Holt City Station (later named Laggan by Lord Strathcona in 1883, then renamed Lake Louise in 1913) was much impressed with the beauty of Lac des Arcs (named by Bourgeau) and he spoke to William Pearce, Superintendent of Mines, about having the government establish a National Parks system. Van Horne said the title of these lands could be in the Canadian Pacific Railway's name, or even his own. Nothing came of Van Horne's efforts in Ottawa in connection with Lac des Arcs. Later he saw the lake at low water, and it was a most depressing sight; for a long time it was laughingly referred to as "Van Horne's Park".

However, William Pearce did take Van Horne seriously in regard to parks, and in 1884 came to the Rockies. He went to the end of track at Mount Stephen, and walked the proposed route. He was disturbed by Van Horne's offer, for fear the Canadian Pacific Railway would develop power plants, at a future date, and destroy the scenery. He recalled that Sir Sandford Fleming had suggested a park after he went through Rogers Pass and was impressed with the beauty of the country.

In 1885, Pearce found Thomas White, Minister of the Interior, sympathetic to the idea of parks. In September, 1885, Pearce visited the hot springs at Banff (Siding 29 was re-named Banff by Lord Strathcona in 1883). Pearce found a raft and wire pulley structure to cross the Bow River just north of the cave. At the cave he found Frank McCabe and William McCardell, employees of the railroad. They showed him a two and a half foot hole with a twenty-foot drop to a pool below. After his descent to the pool and return to the surface, he did not find the two men helpful when he asked the way to the other springs and to Devil's Lake. Indeed, they tried to discourage him. Pearce, however, explored alone, and found out all he needed to know.

White called Pearce to Ottawa in November, 1885. The outcome was the passing, by the Federal Government, on November 25th, of an Order in Council to establish the Banff Hot Springs Reserve (changed in 1887 to the Rocky Mountains Park Reserve), an area of ten square miles around the three Banff hot springs.

It is of interest to note that, as a result of his 1884 and, 1885 trips, Pearce suggested the setting aside of other reserved areas. In time these were to become Yoho, Glacier, and Revelstoke National Parks. The government needed a justification for establishing a park reserve in the Banff area, so White and Pearce suggested a townsite, and a sanitorium along the lines of the European spas, near the springs. This would bring people to Banff; and money to the government's coffers.

Pearce was commissioned by the Federal Government, in 1886, to investigate, report, and make recommendations regarding claims arising at Banff; of alleged prior discoveries of the Hot Springs, of giving publicity to them, and of building improvements at the springs. Previously, Pearce had nailed one hundred placards to trees in the area, warning anyone that the lands around the springs were park reserve and withdrawn from settlement, and that the government would not recognize squatter's rights. William Parkins, Recorder for the Queen's Bench in Manitoba, was appointed to be the secretary for the proceedings.

There were four claimants who argued that they had established certain rights by development: I.G. Grant, Winnipeg, in absentia; D.B. Woodworth, M.P., who claimed a share in McCabe's claim; David Keefe, construction foreman for the Canadian Pacific Railway at Banff Station; McCabe and McCardell, construction men on the Canadian Pacific Railroad. In addition there were three claims by right of prior discovery: D. Theodore Siebring from Donald, British Columbia; Willard E. Young, from Ohio; and Joseph Healy.

Healy waived his claim, but gave evidence. After a comprehensive inquiry into all the evidence, the claims of Young, Grant and Siebring were dismissed on the grounds of no development or no discovery. Keefe had used Company tackle and lumber for the raft, and used the section house as a boarding house without permission; however, he received one hundred dollars for his efforts. Pearce stated if there were any agreement between Woodworth and McCabe it was a civil matter between them. Pearce recommended one thousand dollars for Woodworth, but warned him if he pressed further claims he would be prosecuted for trespass, damage and destruction on Crown land. McCabe and McCardell had filed no claims, but were awarded six hundred and seventy-five dollars for improvements.

Pearce said whoever had built the cabin on the banks of the Bow about 1875 was a possible claimant, but he had not come forward. He also stated that, as a matter of strict justice, no one should have been given any remuneration, but it was thought the easiest way to settle the matter was by a reasonable outlay of cash.

Pearce insisted that the government must have complete control of all park land. Parks were to be developed as recreation areas for the use of the people of Canada, but the government would control all access to the natural resources, and allow them to be developed only if there was no destruction of beauty. Unfortunately, at that time, conservation was secondary to financial gain in the eyes of many government officials.

It may seem that insistence on government control was a very arbitrary action; however, one must remember that the whole idea of parks was very new. The only near examples that Canada had were the American Government Reserves at Hot Springs, Arkansas, and Yosemite Park, and Yellowstone Park, which last showed unhappy results from private ownership. Some Americans wrote saying they hoped Canada would maintain control through the government. The Federal Government was really feeling its way in those early years, and, fortunately, kept its policy flexible enough to meet changing circumstances. People were not yet conscious of parks. Western Canada was little known, settlement was still going westward and most of the west had no settlers, or a very small number. It would be some years before the Canadian Pacific Railway's advertising would bring immigrants. Once started, the development would be very rapid and the prairies would become productive.

In the meantime, this idea of a small park reserve somewhere in the mountains had no real meaning. The government now had control – what were they to do about it? A very small appropriation was conceded by the opposition to be sufficient for development. Fortunately, in 1886, a group of Canadian parliamentarians made a trip across Canada by the new railway to the Pacific coast. Their immediate reaction was that the park should be much larger to save the beauty. They were not unaware of the potential of the mountains to lure international travellers, or of the potential of the hot springs to bring hundreds of invalids to be cured. Doubtless, they saw also the devastation of fires and lumbering.

Likewise, Van Horne said the railroad must not only be paid for but be self-supporting, as well. His idea was to build luxurious hotels in beauty spots such as Banff and Lake Louise to draw the very wealthy to these places. Sportsmen would come for hunting and fishing, and no real mountaineer could resist peaks that had never been climbed. The government had a large investment in the Company's success, and were anxious to cooperate.

In the meantime, industry was still to be a contributing source of income. For some years lumbering and mining were to continue in the Bow River Valley and its tributary valleys. In 1884, the Eau Claire Lumber Company obtained a very large timber berth on the east side of the Spray Valley, which they would work for years to come, and another on Stony Squaw Mountain. As we have seen, Anthracite was a flourishing coal town for a time. At Canmore some surface mining had been done, but, in 1886, coal production began there in earnest, and by 1891, Canmore was a thriving town.

In June, 1887, the Federal Government created the Rocky Mountains Park by Act of Parliament: 'a public park and a pleasure ground for the benefit, advantage and enjoyment of the people of Canada.'

One major factor none of the creators of the park took into consideration was nature, nor could they foresee the problems that would arise when man challenged nature. Floods and forest fires were to cause many worries for park superintendents and it may be well to look into the future, at this point, so that subsequent development of the park and the activities of early superintendents may be better understood.

In 1894 there was an unusual amount of snow, and in May two weeks of very warm temperatures. The snow melted so quickly that the river channel was unable to discharge the water; the overflow was a disaster to property. Roads skirting the river bank were inundated, but bridges in the Banff area, through the vigilance of the government employees, were not damaged by drift timbers. Anthracite suffered greatly, houses and bridges being swept away. Damage to the Canadian Pacific Railway was considerable at that point, as well as at other places in the mountains. This was the worst flood in the short history of the park. The damage to the railway discouraged travellers to a remarkable degree, and there was a considerable falling off of visitors as a natural result. Through trains were stopped in the mountains for weeks, even after the floods subsided. Necessary repairs to tracks and bridges prevented traffic from being carried on satisfactorily. Although flood damage decreased in June and July, the uncertainty lasted through August. In consequence, the Banff Springs Hotel closed earlier than usual because there were virtually no travellers. The flood made the Company realize the life of the railway was threatened, and that greater precautions would have to be taken in the future. Banff business suffered also, though more visiting families than before rented houses for the summer. Because accommodation of this kind was limited, families took turns in using those houses available, or they used tents.

By May, 1902, a bridge, started in March, over the Cascade River was completed to give the visitors a ten mile round trip from Banff along Hoodoo Avenue in the Cascade Valley, across the river by Anthracite and return to Banff by the King Edward VII Highway. Early in May, the whole country was deluged with heavy rain which continued, almost incessantly, through June. The Territories suffered severe damage, with bridges and roads being swept out of existence. In the park, the snow, melting too fast on the mountains, rushed down the narrow channel, carrying drift timber with it. Roads had to be repaired, but, fortunately, the bridges held. Damage to the railway was great, and traffic was suspended for six days, with no travel to east or west. Without doubt, this was the worst flood within anyone's recollection. Possibly, early devastating forest fires were a partial cause of the severe floods. There were no trees left in many places, and the water drained off rapidly into the streams and rivers.

There were other floods through the years but none so destructive as those early ones. When there is heavy snow and sudden melt, the river still overflows its banks. On one occasion in the 1920s, the Bow River flooded the recreation grounds to Cave Avenue and east along it to the bridge. People living along Birch Avenue had to come to the bridge by rowboat. The railway, by then, had taken precautions, and traffic was not disrupted for long periods. Nature on the rampage remains a perpetual problem to the park officials, the railway and the people. Avalanches, heavy snowfalls and landslides still disrupt traffic along the Trans-Canada Highway and the railway, in spite of man's precautions.

Before the railway came, forest fires were started by lightning and by Indians. During the building of the rail line, many fires were started: sometimes deliberately, to clear the way, sometimes accidentally. The sparks from locomotives were a constant source of fires until the Company changed to Diesels. The Company tried to control sparks, but never succeeded completely, and it was necessary to maintain patrols along the line to spot fires. When the park opened, and, as time went on, became a playground for tourists, the fire hazard increased. Hunting, climbing, camping and fishing parties were too often careless about cigar and cigarette butts, and campfires. The story of fires in the parks is a never-ending one. Banff has been endangered many times since 1886. The loss of forests, the destruction of beauty, birds and animals is great in every fire. Moreover, there is often danger to the firefighters, and when fires are really bad, men are taken from their own work, to the detriment of industry.

To list all the fires is not possible here, but a brief account of the major ones will give an idea of the damage incurred in the Park as a result of fire. In 1896, one burned near Laggan (Lake Louise); another, on the northwest side of Mistaya Valley, was started by two prospectors. In 1896, fire almost destroyed the south slopes along the Bow from Vermilion Lakes to beyond Baker Creek. In 1903, the forest from the east gate to Anthracite was destroyed, and the following year, the valley floor from Vermilion Lakes to Baker Creek and well up Johnston Creek. In 1920, twenty fires broke out, and in 1921, twelve fires were fought between Canmore and Lake Louise, one between the Bow River and Glen Avenue, one on Rundle Mountain. In 1930, there were forty fires by the 12th of August, and sixty men fought a fire on the Cuthead toward Palliser. In 1939, on Mt. Rundle near the Devil's Cauldron, three and a half acres burned, and there were thirty other fires by the 23rd of August. It was a very dry year, and Superintendent Jennings closed all trails from the 26th of August to the 5th of September when it rained heavily. These are only a small number of the fires during the years, but one can realize the acreage that has burned in the past. Some were caused by lightning, but the majority by man. In 1969, a bad fire, caused by lightning, destroyed trees from Storm Mountain Lodge to Radium.

The burned areas are now in different stages of grassland, or aspen and lodgepole pine growth; and in the valleys there are willows along rivers, creeks and near marsh areas, but it takes many years for a tree to grow. Years when the sun rises and sets in an angry red-orange glow, when the peaks show dimly through heavy veils of smoke, are bad indeed for the parks in conservation and in business. The warden service is very good, but safety depends on, and is the responsibility of, each person.

IX

A Park
and a Man

The Rocky Mountains Park Act extended the boundaries to a size of 10 by 26 miles, west about seven miles from Banff and east to the foothills beyond Devil's Lake, the whole area being withdrawn from sale of lots. Anthracite was included in the area. It is interesting to note that the act had some preservation clauses, but they could not be very effective at that time because there was too little money. The park was under the Department of the Interior, and the Minister of the Interior had sole authority and control.

George A. Stewart, a Dominion Land Surveyor who had his own business in Winnipeg, was appointed Superintendent in 1886, so he was responsible for the survey and development of the area. The survey was begun in February, 1866, and the townsite was laid out on the north side of the Bow River in a grid form with rectangular lots for businesses and houses to be occupied in the future by residents. It was an unimaginative form of survey though common enough in the west at this time. Banff deserved something better, and more appropriate to its topography and scenic potential. Blocks A and B along the river frontage did not follow the pattern and were larger. The streets were parallel except for Lynx Street (long called Station Road) which ran into Bear Street. On the south side of the Bow, lots were larger and laid out differently, with the idea that they would be 'villa' lots near a fashionable spa. The idea of a spa was very popular at the time. The townsite survey was finished by November 25th.

Preliminary results of the survey showed that roads to reach the Cave and Basin and Upper Hot Springs were a prime necessity. There was only a rough path through the woods that was impossible for invalids to walk to the Cave and Basin. Stewart received instructions in May to open a road from the station to both springs.

The Bow River was a problem – 300 feet wide and deep as well. Time was short, so Stewart decided to build a pontoon bridge as a temporary measure. The first week in June he got men, tools and material.

In the second week the bridge was put together and floated down river to its position (about 200 to 250 yards above the present bridge). By June 12th, it was secured in place at a cost of six hundred dollars.

It was two miles to the station (at 'Old Banff" or 'Siding 29') through scrub, over rough ground and three creeks. As soon as the first road was graded, Stewart put all the men on the road to the Hot Springs. The slope was steep, rising about 700 feet in two and a half miles. The crew had to cut through thick timber and cross gullies, but by July 1st there was a road fit for carriage use. The road, one mile in length, to the Cave and Basin was ready by the middle of July. Stewart then put the men to work on a road from the bridge to Bow Falls and the Spray River.

All winter the men worked on a tunnel into the Cave, where the water flowed out from it. The ladder from the terrace to the pool was impossible for the sick to climb.

During the winter, the Canadian Pacific started excavating for the Banff Springs Hotel, so Stewart had to make a road from the bridge to it. Through thick woods, he managed to complete one that served for heavy teams and wagons. The construction of the hotel started in the spring.

The winter of 1886-1887 was very severe, with heavy snow. Stewart strengthened the bridge and made an opening so logs could be floated through. The lumber companies cut all winter, and when the river opened, floated the logs down to Calgary. Men had to be posted at the bridge to watch, day and night.

A heavy raft, loaded with cordwood, was moored above the bridge to be brought through during the day, and it broke loose. Though it struck the bridge at the centre, the bridge did not break, but a cable on the end parted. The bridge swung on the other cable and landed at the left bank. By using boats, the men were able to hold it until it was secured. Stewart sent a messenger to Calgary, but there was no block and tackle and rope heavy enough available, so he had to send farther east. Several days were lost, then the first rope broke. Yet, after nine days, the bridge was in operation again.

By October of 1887, Stewart had a steel bridge finished, but only after coping with high waters, a twenty mile per hour current, and delays in the shipping of the superstructure materials.

The Cave and Basin presented its own problems, caused by the limestone rock itself. Indeed, when men were working on the outside basin, a whole section of the rock separated and fell into the pool. Stewart put concrete walls around both pools and deepened them, the Cave to four feet and the Basin to five. Control valves were put in both, to control the depth of water. There were additional problems of quicksand and unexpected underground streams. By the time the pools were cleaned of rocks and debris of centuries, it was late autumn of 1887. However, at the Cave and Basin, two rustic, Swiss-style bath houses, built of mountain timber on stone foundations, were ready, one

The Upper Hot Springs, circa 1890.

for ladies, one for gentlemen, separated by the caretaker's house in the centre. All were heated by stoves.

In September of 1887, work started on the road to Devil's Lake, a continuation of Banff Avenue from the station. It was far enough along by the end of October to be finished in the spring. The road ended 300 feet from the lake, leaving space for lodges and hotels when a survey was made.

In the summer of 1886, several sites were applied for at the Hot Springs. Two bath houses were built, one by Dr. R.G. Brett and one by Whitman McNulty. Stewart had to get the water to them, so he built a fifteen foot square reservoir of concrete, connected by pipes and valves to a protective chamber built over the spring outlet. The main supply pipe along the face of the mountain was on a moderate grade. Now there were applications from the Canadian Pacific Railway and Dr. Brett to have the water piped to the Banff Springs Hotel and the Brett Sanitorium Hotel after they had been constructed; the pipe would have a drop of 600 feet with a water pressure of 250 pounds to the square inch. To alleviate the stress, an iron tank was constructed halfway down. The exposed supply pipes were enclosed in wooden casings, packed with moss so temperature loss would not be great. At the Canadian Pacific hotel, the water temperature was 110 degrees Fahrenheit after going through 6,900 feet of pipe; at the Sanitorium, a few degrees less through 8,000 feet.

Neither hotel owner heeded Stewart's warning about the terrific pressure and evidently had a great time with broken pipes in the buildings.

In 1886, Thomas White, Minister of the Interior, sent W.F. Whitcher to the Park Reserve to report on the game and fish in the area. There is no doubt his report affected the Rocky Mountains Park Act passed the next year, and influenced the pattern for control by the government over all park matters. Whitcher suggested wild rice should be planted to encourage wild fowl. The rice came along from Ottawa in 1887, and Stewart had it sown in Vermilion Lakes and on the borders of Devil's Lake (Minnewanka) where it grew very well.

Whitcher said fish should be protected from dynamiting and netting, both of which had killed many fish during the railway construction. He also stated hunting should be prohibited, or species of wild game would disappear. Regarding the latter, Stewart said the Indians were the worst offenders.

Whitcher said good fire protection west of Banff was essential. The valley was badly damaged by fires already, many having started during railway construction, but there was still danger from sparks from locomotives. He suggested that a nursery could be started, and burned areas be replanted from it.

Stewart was much concerned about fires in the summer of 1886, not only because of real danger to the buildings, but because of the time and labour lost. During the following winter, he had men clearing underbrush and fallen trees. This produced firewood, as well as increasing safety and improving the scenery. He let out by contract the cutting of marsh hay, to the west of Banff, which was sold at cost price to teamsters and livery stables, with a dollar royalty per ton for the government; the hay brought in 300 dollars that year.

In 1886, the Park and Banff were a wilderness, but by 1887, there were 650 permanent residents in the park, about 300 of whom were at Anthracite, over 300 in Banff townsite and the rest at the old station. When the Canadian Pacific Railway decided where the new station would be, those people were to move into town. In the townsite were the Brett Sanitorium Hotel on the south side of the river and the Moulton Park Hotel on the north side, and two hotels and one bath house at the Hot Springs. In town, there were boarding houses, two saloons, nine stores, two drugstores, two blacksmith shops, two churches and two post offices, one at Old Banff.

In 1887, Professor Sanders from the Experimental Farm at Ottawa, after a visit to Banff, suggested a nursery with a variety of trees. So in February, 1888, forty thousand trees were ordered from nurseries in the northwestern United States. Twenty thousand of these arrived in May, but the season was late; however, several thousand were planted as suggested at the foot of Cascade Mountain, in ground Stewart had broken for them. The rest he thought would do better in trenches near the river, where there would be more moisture and shelter. The trees were to preoccupy Stewart for three years. The whole experiment was a failure; it was not until many years later that reforestation with local trees was considered.

By 1888, over 5,000 people had used the Cave and Basin, justifying the expense of the year before, to the delight of the Federal Government. The Canadian Pacific hotel, the Banff Springs, had a separate bath house 45 feet x 30 feet, with two compartments, one for ladies, one for gentlemen. There were to be ten tubs and two plunges (small pools with high temperatures), but they were not yet completed. The Sanitorium had ten tubs and two plunges in a detached bath house. At the Hot Springs, A.D. Wright had bought Dr. Bell's bath house and had twelve tubs and a plunge. McCaughy and Beattie had a bath with two tubs and a plunge, and J.W. Brownrigg had one plunge.

The Banff Springs Hotel opened for business on June 1, 1888. The Canadian Pacific Railway decided on the site of the new station which was where the present one stands. The first log station was the one moved from Siding 29; the following year, another log building was built about twenty feet west of it, and the two sections were joined by a covered platform. The people living at the old station site moved to the new townsite, some moving their houses, and by 1897 Siding 29 was gone.

A North West Mounted Police detachment, composed of a police inspector, sergeant, corporal and eight men, occupied tents on Banff Avenue, midway between the old station and the townsite. For winter, a log building was put up on the same site; however, a new location on the west corner of Banff Avenue and Buffalo Street had been chosen for them. When it was ready, the stables would be across the street on Buffalo.

The first Methodist church, where Rundle United now stands, and the first Roman Catholic church, where the Scout Hall is on Lynx Street between Caribou and Wolf Streets, were built in 1887, and the first Presbyterian church, on Bear Street, the following year. The Church of England was using the log town hall, on Bear Street, temporarily, until its church was built.

The following is how a visitor saw it: "A wooden Weslyan Chapel is nearly finished and a site has been selected to build an Episcopalian church. Services are held in the town hall, a humble log and shingle building. The only regular service is conducted in the evening by the Rev. Mr. Williams, a Weslyan missionary, an energetic Welshman. He holds a morning service at Anthracite, a colony of coal miners, about eight miles from Banff. The Episcopalians hold a morning service when they can catch a clergyman and this morning they caught a real live Bishop – the Bishop of Saskatchewan North West Territory. He was accompanied by the Archdeacon, a jolly Irishman, who occupied a front seat at the Weslyan evening service – a not uncommon occurrence."

In 1887, Mr. Carpmael, of the Toronto Observatory, sent temperature and wind recording instruments, and G. McLeod kept the records.

Banff Station in 1888

In the autumn of 1888, the house for the Land Agent was completed, but the Superintendent's was not finished. Mr. Stewart first had his office on Glen Avenue near its junction with River Avenue. Then he moved to Bear Street into a log building where he shared the office with the draftsman, Jacob Smith. A log schoolhouse 24 feet x 24 feet was erected in 1888. At Devil's Lake, the Beach House was built to add to the comfort of the tourists and sportsmen. This log chalet was built by W.J. Astley and W.H. Disbrow and was in operation by 1888.

In 1886, Alf Brown installed phones in the Banff hotels, but they were never connected. In 1889, a telephone system was installed by Mr. Gisborne, on the instructions of the Minister of Public Works. The government office, the police barracks, Hot Springs, Cave and Basin and the Banff Springs Hotel were the first connections, with number one being at the police barracks. Not until many years later was there a long distance line from Banff to Calgary; it was installed by the Alberta Government Telephone Company.

Forest fires in 1889 were worse than for many years, and Banff was threatened more than once. One, which started in the marsh grass northwest of the Bow, endangered Banff, but fortunately for the fire fighters, the wind changed. All summer, police, the government men and the people of the town fought fires. Stewart always had this worry; he cut fire-breaks and cleared dead timber and underbrush whenever he could spare men. He suggested more bridle paths to remote parts of the park to serve as routes of access to fires, as well as being a source of pleasure to visitors. Many visitors who came to Banff liked to camp for a number of weeks, and such trails were cheap to build. Fire in dense timber, in those days, was a terrible thing to fight. Today, with chemicals and plane water-carriers it is desperate enough. All they could do, then, was to watch for sparks, set back-fires and hope a bare mountain peak would act as a barrier against the fire.

Fires had another adverse result. The smoke was so heavy, all through the mountains to the Coast, that many travellers did not stop, and others did not even come to the Rockies. In spite of this, the number of visitors exceeded the previous year.

As long as the weather allowed during the winter of 1889-1890, men were cleaning up rubbish in the burnt-over areas. Then ditches and culverts had to be cleared, as they did every spring; work went forward on the Tunnel Mountain Road, a continuation of Buffalo Street. Much of the dynamiting of the rock had been done late the previous fall. When it was finished, the visitor would have a spectacular drive 500 feet above Bow Falls. A temporary turning place would be made, until further construction would take the road from Tunnel Mountain along the terrace to the Hoodoos. Caribou Street was being continued as a bridle or foot path up the face of Tunnel Mountain, so visitors could reach the top for a magnificent view of the Bow Valley, Devil's Lake and tributary valleys. Early in the season, Disbrow and Ryan put a steam launch on Devil's Lake, and Stewart had a pier and floating bridge built to reach it.

The government decided a Land Agent was not needed in Banff and recommended that Stewart move into the agent's house on Buffalo Street, the site of the Superintendent's house until the 1960s. The government said the unfinished house being built for Stewart should be converted to a Museum, and Stewart had work started on that. Stewart told the government electric lights would help, and wondered if there was some way to use the pressure of the sulphur water.

An amendment was made to the Park Act to bring hunting in the park area under strict government control. Stewart took the view that the rivers and lakes were good for the propagation of fish, but that there should be stringent game laws to preserve wild animals and fowl. No appropriation was made to pay for a warden, however, nor would there be for some years to come.

Every year the meteorological report was kept by Mr. McLeod, though his other duties were too heavy after July 1st for it to be complete. His house location was fine for temperature records, but poor for wind direction readings. Professor Carpmael had suggested the top of Sulphur Mountain was the best spot for a wind instrument, showing velocity and direction. Stewart reported that the visitors were always inquiring about these yearly weather conditions.

From these few incidents of the first years of Banff, it must be clear that George Stewart had a stupendous task. Virtually unaided, he had to hew, blast, ditch and drain a wilderness. It was difficult to place the interests of the visitors first. He endeavoured to keep government buildings rustic to suit the park. He planted trees on Main Street and by the river. 'Beautify' the government said, but it provided very little money to Stewart for this purpose. Stewart used labour and materials at hand; he was constantly improvising. He planned future improvements, he asked for fire wardens, he urged an extension of park boundaries – all of which were necessary, but all of which required funds.

Banff was in an isolated position in those days, and the railway was the only line of communication. If materials were needed, a message had to go to Calgary, and often farther. Calgary, itself, was still a very small place, not even the size Silver City had been in its hey-day.

Instructions from the Department of the Interior had to be followed; visiting personages had to be welcomed and entertained. Stewart was Superintendent, surveyor, town planner (even choosing the future site of the cemetery), arbitrator, and liaison between the people and the government. Later, he would have to be Justice of the Peace.

However, one must give the Federal Government its due. It was trying to cope with a completely new situation. The park was a long distance from Ottawa, and most of the parliamentarians had no idea of its physical difficulties. They realized the potential of the tourist business; they could do nothing else, considering the number of visitors and resultant income. However, the park seemed to cost a lot of money – in 1890 the expenditure was $11,498.38. Most of the members of the House of Commons had vague ideas about the park as a place where the "natural unchanged beauty" must be preserved for "the pleasure of the people of Canada". How could this be with forest fires, mining, lumbering, and quarrying going on within its borders? The difficulty was they did not realize the destruction of beauty by fire and industry – and industry did bring in money.

The government's park policy in those early years was very flexible. Stewart was given a free hand. Situations were met as they arose. The government's suggestions may not always have been practicable, but they were well meant. Ignorance of the real problems and the absence of guidelines to follow explain most of the government's shortcomings. Later, that very flexibility which was so useful and essential to George Stewart and Howard Douglas, who followed him, was to bring new problems to the Park and its people.

George A. Stewart, the first Park Superintendent.

Pearce in a letter to Tom Wilson wrote the following: "There is one thing... in connection with the laying out of Banff... The man that should be given the credit for the laying out of footpaths, bridle-paths, and roadways there ... is the Surveyor-General, now Dr. Deville. The Surveyor-General obtained instruments from France, necessary to determine distance and elevations. The system devised was by running lines about 200 feet apart at right angles to the river and as high up as was thought that foot-paths etc. could be established. [This system, as noted earlier, did not realize the full potential of the site.]

"Mr. Stewart's son was given charge of that work so far as getting data on the ground etc. and he did the work admirably. The maps were prepared by my friend Jacob Smith... Having these maps prepared it was the simplest matter... to take a hatchet and blaze out the necessary route."

Pearce also commented that Stewart took all the credit, that he was not diplomatic, and that friction developed in Banff He also wrote that Stewart's superior officers ignored this because they felt it advisable to support him at that time.

On the other hand, it would seem Stewart deserved credit for what he accomplished. Anyone who has tried to clear a small area of trees, let alone a townsite, knows the work it is. Drawing lines on paper is one thing – in the forest, with primitive tools and few men, it is another.

As far as "friction" is concerned, Stewart found himself squeezed between the government in Ottawa and the people in Banff. He had orders to open a townsite, develop the Hot Springs and make the park productive. It is doubtful if the government had any ideas how this was to be done. Pearce admits in his letter that he had been asked to report secretly to the government about the progress made by Stewart. It was a kind of a spy role which he did not relish. From the tone of the letter one would gather there could have been a personal animosity.

The people of Banff, growing in number with the frontier town, were frequently ignored by the government in those days. The very flexibility of government policy was developing a spirit of independence and free thinking in those residents. Their isolation had already developed their self-sufficiency, both socially and politically.

X

The New Century

Banff, from its inception, has been unique. The name itself, bestowed on a siding of the railroad, was a whim of Lord Strathcona. Banff was not discovered, the hot springs were. The Banff Hot Springs Reserve was created by Order in Council. Then Rocky Mountains Park came into being by Act of Parliament.

The townsite was a necessity, to provide for the visitors who would come to the spa. The Federal Government, from the beginning, controlled the land. The government had to promote quick settlement and investment to appease the opposition. It quickly bought back any lots that were sold on land not in the reserve, and no squatter's rights were recognized. Arguments in Parliament were numerous: might leasing lead to political patronage? Was it right to spend public money for the enjoyment of the wealthy visitors? So questioned the opposition. On it's side, the government said it would have control of land use and prevent commercial exploitation by individual ownership.

How long should a lease last, and should it be renewed, were other questions. Twenty-one years was suggested, but Sir John A. Macdonald said no individual would build an expensive residence for twenty-one years, so there must be the right to renew. The government agreed, and residential lots were issued, with a renewable 'in perpetuity' or 'and so on forever' clause, at a fixed annual rental for the first forty-two years at the end of which time a review of the lease would be issued. A suitable building would have to be built, and the use for which the land was intended would have to be stated. Nothing of a noisy or offensive nature to other residents was to be allowed. No leases were to be transferred without government permission. Land rent would vary according to lot size, location and use; at that time the range was roughly two and a half to ten dollars per year. This was acceptable to the residents in the 1880s, with the exception of a small number who held out for squatter's rights, but to no avail. As business changed in the park, the question of leases was to become a very pertinent and persistent problem.

Though the townsite was surveyed, the efforts of the government were first extended to roads and other public works for the visitors' pleasure. Only Banff Avenue, between Buffalo and Caribou Streets, and Bear Street and Caribou Street were cleared for business and houses. Later, Banff Avenue was cleared to Wolf, which was also cleared; then Beaver Street was started.

Not only government policy was to influence the development of Banff. The Canadian Pacific Railway was a real influence in its growth and developments. The railway company had to make money. It had to have travellers. Van Horne's idea was to appeal to the tastes of the moneyed-class. After all, in those days it was only the wealthy who travelled for pleasure. In Canada, only a few Easterners were well-to-do and could afford such luxury; in the west, people were just starting business. The wealthy of Europe, the British Isles and the United States, who wanted something new and different, were Van Horne's targets. So the Canadian Pacific Railway's thinking agreed with the government's, when it came to quick development. One of the first roads to be made usable was the one from the station to the Banff Springs Hotel, so building materials could be transported quickly.

The Company's influence is seen in the ready government help given in the same way to Dr. R.G. Brett, who was the Company doctor on the railway construction line and who had the monetary help of the Canadian Pacific Railway Company to build the Brett Sanitorium and Grand View Villa Hotels. Dr. Brett was also the Company doctor for the park. His lease for the Sanitorium Hotel (later 'Sanitarium Hotel' and still later 'Bretton Hall Hotel') was one of the first issued. In later years, he became Lieutenant-Governor of Alberta, but his home was in Banff, built on his hotel grounds facing Spray Avenue. The old hotel stood where the Administration Buildings are today. For many years, Dr. Brett looked after the ailments of the Banff people. He was the typical old time doctor and a clever one as well. A sick visit was a social visit. After seeing the patient, he always had time to sit down and enjoy a cup of tea and a piece of cake, his favourite being fruitcake. He would chat with the family, then be on his way. He was a fine gentleman with polished manners and a kind heart. He was popular as Lieutenant-Governor and was loved by the people of Banff. Of course, he loved a dollar – but who doesn't – and he did enjoy a political argument.

Canadian Pacific patronage and, for many years, government patronage, was also extended to the Brewster family which obtained a virtual monopoly of the transport business in both Banff, and later, Jasper Parks. Patronage has always existed in Banff, in one form or another, and various people have used it to further their own ends.

Canadian Pacific advertising in the early years made Banff known the world over. The Canadian Pacific hotels: Banff Springs, Chateau Lake Louise, Mount Stephen House at Field, and Glacier House were famous for their great fireplaces, luxurious lounges, fine service and wonderful meals. A visitor, staying at the Banff Springs Hotel in 1894, wrote: "The building is high. There is only one thing higher in the attractive concern which is the price of the liquor. In every other feature it is unsurpassed." All travellers agreed the hotel settings were "beautiful and the scenery unsurpassed". Another guest said of the hotel, "It contains corridors for the invalid, turrets for the astronomer and balconies for the lovers."

The Canadian Pacific Railway depended on Anthracite and Canmore for coal. Then Anthracite was closed. The Company began to look around and, by 1902, had a license of occupancy, covering 7,360 acres of coal land in Rocky Mountains Park, near Cascade Mountain, along the road to Devil's Lake. Donald Bogart Dowling, an engineer in the Canadian Geological Survey Department, explored the Cascade Coal Basin. His work was in coal, petroleum and natural gas. In 1933, the Canadian Institute of Mining and Mineralogy, of which he was a member from 1904 to 1925, erected the cairn at the east end of Banff Avenue, where the road turns north to the traffic circle, in recognition of his work in the area.

Operations at the mine began in 1903, and a railway spur was run to it. By 1904, a new townsite had come into the park. Bankhead was built on the upper terrace north of the mine and was a company town. It started with forty houses, two large boarding houses, offices with a mess hall above for office staff and heads of departments, and a house for the superintendent of the mine, D.G. Wilson. There were, also, the Roman Catholic church, a four room school and a hall used for concerts or religious services of other denominations.

Bankhead had recreational facilities for hockey, skating, baseball and tennis. A company store was operated by White and Bayne. Benny Fay ran the butcher shop. Bankhead had sewers, water and light before Banff did. The population of 600 was 75 percent immigrant German, Polish, Italian and Chinese (because only Chinese would work in the tipple).

The coal at Bankhead was very high in heat value and good for domestic or industrial use, but not for locomotives. As in the Anthracite mine, the coal was very friable, so the briquette plant was started in 1907, and briquettes were used for locomotives and domestic heating. Pitch was brought from Sault Ste. Marie which added to production costs. Demand varied summer to winter, so large storage space was necessary. This was the first briquette plant in the West. In 1909, there was a World Fair in Seattle, and the Canadian Pacific had one hundred boxes of briquettes stamped "Banff Hard Coal", which were distributed at the Fair.

The mine, in competition with Drumheller, Lethbridge and Canmore, never operated at peak capacity. 1913 was its best operating year in production and sale price. In 1911, there was a strike for higher wages. Another strike, which lasted eight months in 1922, was only one of many all over Canada at the time, but faced with high production costs and competition from other

Coal-mining at Bankhead.

mines, including the one at Canmore, the Company decided to give up the Bankhead operation.

The briquette plant ran for eighteen more months. When it finally closed, all the buildings were moved to Canmore, Calgary or Banff. The houses sold for fifty dollars per room, and some of the buildings are still in Banff. The miners went to other mines; many of the office and store people came to Banff to make their homes. Who but the Canadian Pacific Railway could have obtained permission to open up such a mining development in a park? The isolation of Banff and the government's need for help in its development made the Canadian Pacific a strong political force for many years.

The Banff residents were willing to go along with both the government and the Canadian Pacific Railway. After all, they, too, had to earn a living. They worked for the government on the many jobs the superintendent always had available. They had work as drivers of democrats or tally-hos for the visitors. They worked at the Banff Springs Hotel or on the railway. Many became outfitters, guides and packers for the visitors who wanted to go on climbing, hunting, fishing and exploring expeditions. These guides, men such as Walter and Bill Peyto, Frank and Jim Tabiteau, Sid Unwin, Tom Wilson, Bill and Jim Brewster, Ralph Edwards, Jim Simpson, George Harrison and many others, became well known to early travellers. Mountaineers, explorers, botanists and geologists came back year after year; each had his favourite guide and packer. Their trips would be planned ten to twelve months in advance. The visitors had their favourite horses for riding as well as the ones in the pack train. These animals, for their sagacity, their tricks, their lovableness, and their sheer cussedness, fill many pages in the books written about the Rockies.

Other residents had general stores where the traveller could buy trail outfits, from boots to hats, and, through the guide, food for a trip. Thus the Banff people earned a living one way or another from both the government and the railway, as well as the visitors.

Many changes were to come to Rocky Mountains Park as the government's policy developed. One of the changes important to park development was the seemingly frequent boundary change. In 1892, 51 miles x 54 miles were set aside around Lake Louise as a forest reserve. In 1902, this reserve was incorporated into Rocky Mountains Park, the boundaries of which were extended to include the watershed of the Bow River. The area of the park was now over 3,000 square miles.

Lake Louise had been discovered by Tom Wilson in 1882.[1] Late in 1889, William Whyte (later Sir William) of the Canadian Pacific Railway asked W.J. Astley of Banff if he would go to Lake Louise and make arrangements for a chalet to be built by the Company's carpenters. The year before, when Tom Wilson cut a trail to the lake, John Enselwood, a Canadian Pacific employee, was in charge of a crew who built a lean-to shack, near the present swimming pool, to be used by fishermen as a shelter. Dave White may have helped with the construction; it is possible as a boat of his was left there for fishermen. The log chalet that Astley managed had a lounge, a kitchen, two bedrooms, an attic and a verandah. This chalet burned down in 1891. Astley received instructions to build a larger chalet, rustic Swiss style, and he chose

---

[1] In 1882 a Stony Indian took Tom Wilson in to the 'Lake of Little Fishes' (Lake Louise). Being the first white man to see it, Wilson replaced the Indian name with 'Emerald Lake'. In 1883, Dr. G.M. Dawson visited the lake with Wilson, who says he cut a trail through at that time. On his map in 1886, Dawson marked it as 'Emerald Lake'. Wilson said he took Mrs. James Ross, wife of Chief of Construction for C.P.R. mountain section, and Mrs. Brothers, wife of superintendent of coast division, into the lake, and they were the first white women to see Lake Louise. (Wilson gives no date.) Wilson goes on to say the name was changed to 'Louise' by Dawson when Louise, daughter of Lord Mount Temple, President of the British Medical Association, visited Laggan in 1884. (This, in a letter by J.A. Jaffray, Jan. 19, 1929 to W.J. Astley – in the Archives of the Canadian Rockies.) Others say a railway worker took her into the lake. Alberta Provincial Librarian, Jaffray writes: 'Wilson said Dawson took her.' In the *Trail Blazer of the Canadian Rockies* p.30 by Tom Wilson as told to W. Round, Wilson says the Geographical Society (Geographic Board?) named the lake and Dawson was not in to it. *Place Names of Alberta* issued by the Geographic Board of Canada 1928 indicates it was named after Princess Louise Caroline Alberta, daughter of Queen Victoria and wife of the Marquis of Lorne, Governor General of Canada 1878-83, and named by Hindman (also Hyndman), a surveyor who worked on the C.P.R. with Rogers. The editors of *2000 Place Names of Alberta 1972*, E.J. Holmgren and P.M. Holmgren, wisely state only that it was named for Princess Louise. I offer this explanation to show how disputes over names of these early places arise. Wilson was not a young man when W. Round wrote. At least one thing is beyond dispute – the name is 'Lake Louise'.

the site where the present Chateau stands. In charge until late 1896, Astley then moved to Nelson, British Columbia. He had laid out and supervised the building of the first wagon trail from Laggan along the creek to the lake and he named Lake Annette for his mother.

In 1886, an Order in Council initiated by William Pearce provided for park sites along the Canadian Pacific railroad to preserve the forest beauty: ten miles square at Mount Stephen; twenty miles square at Mount Sir Donald including the railway loop and ten miles square at Glacier; nineteen miles square at Eagle Pass, including Mount Griffen and the three valley lakes. This last was abolished in 1902 when half of it was sold for timber. 'Miles square' were changed to 'square miles' the following year.

As the steep grade of the Big Hill at Field made pulling the additional weight of dining cars difficult, a lunch-room stop was discussed in 1886. The Canadian Pacific used a dining car on a siding until 1887, when Mount Stephen House and Glacier House were opened. At Glacier, the first building, adjacent to the station, was rectangular, with a kitchen, dining room, reception room and six bedrooms, and had a staff of ten. Mr. H.A. Perley was the first manager, followed by the Misses Mollison, and in 1893, Mrs. Julia Mary Young took over until she retired in 1920. Trains stopped at 12:50 p.m. and 2:20 p.m., when a half hour was allowed for lunch. In 1889, Glacier House was enlarged, and by 1906, an adjacent annex ran up the valley giving ninety more rooms, baths and elevators. Glacier House was famous for its home-like atmosphere, its meals and its wine.

In 1903, the government increased the area of the Selkirk Reserve to 700 square miles, administered by the Superintendent of Rocky Mountains Park. In the same year, Deutschman discovered the Nakimu Caves at Glacier, and the government began a limited development. Trails to Beaver Valley, Illecilliwaet Glacier, Asulkan Valley, Marion Lake and Avalanche Crest were opened as day trips. Glacier House was the centre from which everything was directed. W.S. Ayers, mining engineer, Parks Department, was sent to survey the caves. Deutschman lived in a log hut, roofed with cedar shakes, and served as guide to the caves. He discovered two more caves in 1920, and the government tried to improve the accessibility to all of them by stairways, guardrails and lighting.

The Canadian Pacific Railway made Glacier a supplement to Banff by offering a combined tour. They advertised the Rockies and Selkirks with the real emphasis on unclimbed peaks, glaciers, and untouched valleys. It was a period of great mountaineering and rising scientific interest in geology, botany and glaciation. The elite travelled for pleasure, for exploration and scientific reasons. They measured heights of peaks (A.P. Coleman determined the true heights of Mounts Brown and Hooker, which had intrigued mountaineers since the time of Douglas); they discovered ice fields (J.N. Collie discovered the Columbia Ice Field in 1898) and collected specimens of flowers. Botanical books were written, such as those by John Macoun and Julia Henshaw, and that of Mr. Stewardson Brown and Mrs. Mary Schaffer. The mountaineers discovered and named new mountains and lakes; they mapped the country; they studied the geology and fossil beds. Some of the well known climbers whose names appeared again and again in the registers at Banff, Lake Louise and Glacier Hotels were: C.E. Fay, James Outram, J.W.A. Hickson, Mrs. M. Schaffer, E.W.D. Holway, F.K. Butters, Howard Palmer, L.W. Longstaff, W.S. Green, H.W. Topham, Walter Wilcox, S.E.S. Allen, P.S. Abbot, H.E.M. Stutfield, J.N. Collie, George and W.S. Vaux, who also made many observations of glaciation over five years, and their sister Mary Vaux, who painted wild flowers. The mountain climbing, scientific and travel books of all these people had worldwide circulation and gave much publicity to the Banff area.

Mountaineering in the park has had its tragic side. In 1896, P.S. Abbot plunged to his death from above Death Trap Col (later named Abbot Pass) in his attempt to climb Mount Lefroy at Lake Louise. In 1921, Dr. W.E. Stone and his wife set out so he could climb Mount Eon. That he succeeded in making the first ascent of the peak is known because he had built a cairn there; but he was never to tell of it because he must have stepped on a loose slab of rock to fall hundreds of feet to his death. Rudolph Aemmer, a Swiss guide; Walter Peyto and Walter Child, wardens; and a Royal Canadian Mounted Policeman found Mrs. Stone stranded on a ledge eight days later. Aemmer reached her, and she was raised by a rope. Then Aemmer carried her on his back two miles up and down Mount Eon and along its base to a bivouac at timberline, to rest before she could be taken farther.

Tragedies such as these are unusual, and were not the result of carelessness. Some later tragedies, actually very few in number, resulted when people persisted in climbs in spite of warnings, or went off without notifying the wardens. Considering the great number of famous ascents and more general climbs, tragedies in the parks were, and are, rare.

Unusual things have happened in the mountains. Jim Simpson told me that he was lost one time in a deep valley of heavy timber in the Athabasca River region. He said he was completely disoriented when a stranger appeared and beckoned to Jim to follow. Jim, having nothing to lose, did so and reached his camp, but turning to thank him saw the stranger had gone. Norman Luxton told me about a goat hunt he went on with Frank and Howard Sibbald, Tom Lusk, Jim Simpson and Bill Brewster. Moses Bear, the Indian with them, and Norman Luxton were hunting the high ridges west of Peyto Lake. Norman was crossing to another ridge when a rock slide started, and he was being carried down by the slide when a stranger came to his assistance. Some hours later the stranger and Norman came within sight of the camp fire, and then – the stranger was gone. Norman found his friends holding a wake for him, Moses having told them that Norman had been buried. Miss Elizabeth Rummel told me that when she used to go in to Skoki it was often sunshine below, but when she reached Deception Pass, there could be a real whiteout with a blizzard. She had to reach the camp and going along, alone and almost blinded, she would hear Paley's skis swishing through the snow beside her. In 1933, Dr. R.E. Paley had been buried in a snow slide which extended, on the southeast slope, from Fossil Mountain to Baker Lake. Other men who used to climb alone have told me they have heard beautiful music for which there was no explanation.

From the beginning, artists have found Banff, Yoho and Glacier National Parks places of pictures without end. Captain Henry J. Warre was probably the first visiting artist near the Banff area. In 1845, he painted Cascade Mountain from Canmore, as well as other peaks in the vicinity, and a very large panoramic view of the mountains and foothills from the Bow River. In 1881, Sydney Prior Hall, a special artist for the *London Graphic* magazine, travelled west in the party of the Marquis of Lorne and did pencil drawings of the mountains and foothills. In 1887, Lucius R. O'Brien, who was the first president of the Canadian Art Academy, did a very fine painting of Temple Mountain near Lake Louise.

Sidney Vick was probably the first artist who lived in Banff; and he was followed by others who lived here or had summer homes. John D. Curren lived in Cochrane and painted some interesting historical pictures of the Banff area. Nicholas de Grandmaison, one of the greatest of Indian portrait painters, has had his home in Banff for many years. Another who lived in Banff was W.J. Phillips of woodcut and water colour fame. Carl Rungius, premier animal painter; Belmore Browne, noted for his scenic oils; and his son George Browne, noted for painting game birds, all came to their summer homes to paint in the park. Gerda Christoffersen and Dorothy Oxborough are known for their Indian portraits. Mrs. Norah Drummond Davis, the eccentric, who painted for Raphael Tuck & Sons in England before coming here to do wild animals or historic scenes, called Banff 'home'. Peter Whyte, a native son of Banff, noted for his variety of subjects and versatile style, grew to manhood in these mountains. Over the years there have been many visiting artists, each indulging in his own field: John Innis and Rolland Gissing, Mrs. Doyle (sister of Mrs. Drummond Davis), Annora Brown, W. Langdon Kihn, R.H. Palinsky and Alfred C. Leighton, among others.

Sculptors, too, visited Banff, but Charlie Beil, a one time student of Charles Russell, stayed. Like those of his great teacher, his bronzes, in dioramas or as single pieces and trophies, are world famous. Sonia de Grandmaison executes bronze busts of dignitaries, and Ella Mae Walker of Edmonton sculptured Indian busts.

Photographers there were and are without number, but W. Hanson Bourne was the first resident photographer; he arrived in 1893, and produced Indian photographs which are collectors' items. Then came Byron Harmon

A group outside Norman Luxton's Sign of the Goat shop, Banff, 1911.

from Olympia, Washington, in 1904; he stayed and rose from baby and passport photos to world fame with his scenic photographs of the mountains. The story goes that Harmon set up a photographic business after pretending to take a photograph of his first customer and asking for a deposit before developing it. With the deposit he rushed out and bought a film – there had been nothing in his camera – then he returned and told his customer he would like to retake the 'picture'. Now he really was in business! His first shop was in the Mackay and Dippie Building, next to Rundle United Church on Banff Avenue. In 1909, he bought Moore's Livery Stable, where Monod's shop stands in the Harmony Block. The Harmony Theatre stood where the Chinese Cafe had been in earlier days. When he rebuilt after the fire (1917) he owned the Harmony Drug Store, a gift shop and a fountain lunch. In 1911, Harmon became the official photographer on an exploratory expedition into the Mount Robson area; A.O. Wheeler was surveyor, Conrad Kain, guide, and Don Phillips was packer and cook. This expedition was backed by the railways, the Alberta and British Columbia Governments and the Dominion Government for the purpose of opening up the country. The party climbed thirty peaks from 7,000 feet to over 11,000 feet above sea level. In 1925, Harmon took photographs of the Columbia Ice Fields for the *National Geographic Magazine*. He travelled for the National Parks when Commissioner J.B. Harkin was carrying on an advertising campaign at World

Fairs and Expositions. Byron Harmon's pictures became world famous and did much for the western National Parks by making them better known.

In addition to the mountaineers and explorers who wrote about Rocky Mountains Park, some Banff people wrote of their experiences. Mary Schaffer Warren, Dan McCowan, Earle Birney, Walter J. Phillips and Ralph Edwards were among others. These people wrote of their experiences, and their works show the influence of the mountains. Dan McCowan's books reflect much of the wild life, while in the others, pack-trip experiences play a part. Earle Birney in his poem *David* shows even more clearly the influence of the natural surroundings.

In the 1920s, the beauty of the scenery inspired W.R. Round to write the lyrics and music for *Lake Minnewanka* and *The Setting of the Sun.* Likewise, Mort Green wrote the lyrics for Harry Revel's music *When There's A Breeze on Lake Louise* for the RKO Radio Motion Picture *The Mayor of 44th St.,* in 1942.

Members of various royal families have visited Banff and the Parks, since the days of phaetons drawn by matched horses. For them, Banff became a place to stay and rest, without formal public appearances. Kings, queens, princes and princesses have always been allowed to drive or to walk, to enjoy the natural beauty with no overt fuss, and many of these Royal visitors have been recipients of hospitality in private homes.

When His Majesty King George VI and Her Majesty Queen Elizabeth were visiting Banff in 1939, the King saw the Union Jack flying on the top of Sulphur Mountain.

His Majesty asked, "Who placed the Union Jack there?"

Major Jennings, the Superintendent, replied, "Mr. Sanson put it there in honour of your visit. Would you like to meet him?"

Mr. Norman Sanson was presented, and presently the King said, "I like the flag there."

Whereupon Major Jennings said, "It shall remain there until the winds and storms have worn it to shreds." – which it did.

In 1897, Peter Sarbach, from Switzerland, came with a British climbing party, and he was the first Swiss guide in the Canadian Rockies. In 1899, the Canadian Pacific Railway brought out Edward Feuz, Senior, and Christian Hasler, Senior, certified guides. In the autumn they went back to Interlaken and returned to Canada in the spring. Christian Bohren and Edward Feuz, Junior, joined them in 1903; Gottfried Feuz in 1906; Rudolf Aemmer and Ernest Feuz in 1909; Christian Hasler, Junior, in 1912. That year some of the guides brought their families with them; they lived at Glacier for the winter and were the first skiers in the western mountains. Then the Swiss village, 'Edelweiss', was built on the steep slope, one half mile from Golden, and they moved there. Not until 1920 did the Canadian Pacific build a guides' house at Lake Louise where Edward Rudolf and Ernest and Walter Feuz

Their majesties King George VI and Queen Elizabeth, with J.I. Brewster driving.

had quarters. Christian Hasler, Junior, used to do road work in winter and he stayed at Glacier until 1925. The later generation guides had Canadian Pacific hotel contracts.

The Connaught Tunnel, finished in 1916, was built to avoid avalanches, and Glacier House stood in isolation. Macdonald Station and Avalanche Village were moved to a new site at the west portal of the tunnel. The government built a new road from the station to Glacier House, but in 1925, the Canadian Pacific closed it. After the rails were taken up, not as many people went to stay at Glacier House. Finally, in 1929, a Calgary contractor bought the windows, doors, stoves, pipes and rods. Then the Canadian Pacific burned Glacier House down.

Rogers Hut, the first climbers' hut in the area that the Canadian Pacific had built at the foot of the glacier and that Christian Hasler and Ernest Feuz kept repaired for many years, was the last to go when it finally collapsed under the weight of snow. The traveller can still see the remains of the old railway grade as he drives over Rogers Pass.

Tom Wilson had looked down into Yoho Valley in 1882, and fifteen years later he told Professor Jean Habel from Germany about it. The Professor explored the valley, and as a result the government expanded the Mount Stephen reservation to 800 square miles in 1901, and named it Yoho Park. It came under the administration of the Superintendent of Rocky Mountains Park.

XI

Park Policy

George A. Stewart was Superintendent until 1896, when he was removed by Order in Council and went to Calgary to work in a government department there. When the Liberal party came to power that year, Howard Douglas was appointed and remained in office until 1908, when A.B. Macdonald became Superintendent.

Stewart and Douglas were the two men who really moulded Rocky Mountains Park and Banff for nearly twenty-five years. They had to get permission and instructions from Ottawa; but at a time when control was flexible, they were given wide powers and made responsible for development and administration. Both men were accused of favouritism toward certain people and became unpopular with some of the town residents; however, a precedent had been set when the government allowed the Canadian Pacific Railway so much freedom in its activities in the park. These two men, like the Federal Government, were anxious to achieve results. To get a thing done was more important than who did it. All concerned wanted good financial returns and improved facilities for visitors in housing, comforts, trails and roads. The town and the park were dependent on the scenery, hot springs and tourists for their existence. For many years, the superintendents had to encourage lumbering, mining, and quarrying to bring in money; yet, strangely enough, both men were aware of conservation. At first, the park area was small, and it was hard to encourage the visitor to fish and to hunt, and at the same time, to preserve game. If a man had to walk or ride only a few miles to the park boundary to do either, the fish and game were bound to suffer; both superintendents kept urging the government to extend the boundaries as a game reserve. Likewise, they repeatedly requested help to control forest fires. Stewart and Douglas were men anxious for the success of

Rocky Mountains Park and its future, and though they did things primarily for the visitor, that very motivation aided the preservation of the park's natural riches.

the East Gate of Rocky Mountains Park, circa 1920

Rocky Mountains Park was like an orphan child for years; no government department wanted the administrative responsibility for its development. From 1887 to 1908, Rocky Mountains Park and park reserves were administered from Ottawa by the Deputy Minister of the Interior, assisted by a Departmental Secretary and a Deputy Law Clerk. Local administration of the park and the reserves was in the hands of the superintendent at Banff.

In 1908, the park and park reserves came under the Department of Forestry, which brought the park aim of conservation into conflict with the idea of forest exploitation. That same year, Superintendent H. Douglas was promoted to become Commissioner of Parks, with an office in Banff until 1910. Then the Commissioner was sent to Edmonton to be closer to the Jasper Park development. In 1911, Douglas became Chief Superintendent of Parks and was responsible for the superintendents in the western parks and reserves. He retired in 1912, but the office continued until 1917.

A Conservation Commission was appointed in 1909 to consider fire and game protection. To make warden patrol possible, the area of Rocky Mountains Park was decreased by almost half in 1911. In 1917, the boundaries were extended to include the Red Deer and Clearwater Rivers to preserve the breeding grounds of the wild animals.

In 1911, the Honourable Frank Oliver, Minister for the Department of Interior, succeeded in having the Dominion Forest Reserves and Parks Act passed. This was important because it created the Dominion Parks Branch in the Department of Forestry; this branch was to continue for ten years. The same Act separated Yoho and Glacier parks from Rocky Mountains Park, each with its own superintendent, warden and staff.

To head this new Dominion Parks Branch, Commissioner James B. Harkin was appointed by Order in Council, August, 1911. From 1911 to 1936, J.B. Harkin was to have as great an influence on park policy as George A. Stewart and Howard Douglas had. Preservation of the environment and conservation of wild life in the parks, as well as tourism, were to become primary concerns of J.B. Harkin. It happened that he came into control when preservation and conservation were issues of international, as well as national, importance. People had suddenly become aware of scenic beauty and wilderness values. The automobile was becoming more and more popular. Then, too, the economy in the pre-1914 years was buoyant; not only the people, but the government had more money to spend. The Boer War had ended in 1902, and labour was plentiful; the financial crisis of the 1890s in the United States was over.

Harkin, a native of Vankleek Hill, Ontario, had his early education there and finished it in Marquette, Michigan. In 1892, he started as a newspaper man in Montreal, going, the next year, to work for the *Ottawa Journal*. Very soon, he rose to the position of city editor and had access to the Parliamentary Press Gallery. In 1901, the Honourable Clifford Sifton needed a political secretary and he asked P.D. Ross, the editor-owner of the *Ottawa Journal*, if he knew anyone suitable. Ross recommended Harkin who, in December, 1901, became a first class clerk. In February, 1904, by Order in Council, he became the Minister's Private Secretary, but was not transferred to the staff of the Department of the Interior until 1907.

When the Honourable Mr. Sifton retired in 1905, the Honourable Frank Oliver asked Harkin to stay on, so he was Private Secretary until 1911. Harkin, now experienced in policy and administration under the Minister for the Interior, was given the choice of supervising federal water power development or of being in charge of administration of the national parks. He chose the latter, and after the Act was passed, he was appointed Commissioner for Dominion Parks by Order in Council, in August, 1911. He had a small staff, partly from the Department of Forestry Branch, which had administered the parks since 1908, partly from the Dominion Surveys Branch, and some others with special training.

Harkin, after touring the west, realized to the fullest extent the potential wealth of the parks. He saw the need for more roads to make the parks accessible because he could foresee what the automobile would mean to tourism. By stressing the money tourists would bring, he succeeded in getting large appropriations for the Parks Branch. This was John Harkin's beginning, and reading the following pages, one will realize what he accomplished.

Park Superintendent Howard Douglas (extreme right) entertains J.A. Sifton (facing camera) at a picnic, circa 1900.

J.B. Harkin, a man with wide knowledge and vision, was dedicated to his work. He had a pleasing manner and an even disposition which made him respected by his staff. He deliberated, then decided. He also had very strong convictions about parks, public recreation, conservation and history as related to the Canadian people.

In 1936, the four Federal Government Departments of Mines, Indian Affairs, Immigration and Colonization, and the Interior were amalgamated by Parliament, leaving a surplus of senior officials. This meant Harkin would have to report to the Minister through a Director responsible not only for National Parks, but also for administering forestry, public lands and Canada's northland. Harkin refused the position of Controller of the National Parks Bureau and retired at sixty-one years of age. Mount Harkin in Kootenay Park and a bronze tablet on the Administration Building grounds in Banff, erected in 1958 by the National Parks Services, are visible memorials to him. Mr. Harkin was in office through six different changes of administration, from Conservative to Liberal, a noteworthy testimony of his ability. Usually, when a new party came into power, there would be a changeover among civil servants.

Just six years before he retired, one of Harkin's ambitions was realized when the National Parks Act was passed in 1930, removing the parks from the jurisdiction of the Department of Forestry. The Natural Resources Act gave back to the four western provinces the remaining Crown Lands, except within the boundaries of the national parks which would remain under federal legislative jurisdiction. The park boundaries were resurveyed to follow more natural divisions. Banff National Park was to go north to the watershed at Sunwapta Pass and include the upper Siffleur and Clearwater Rivers. The Red Deer, Ghost and Kananaskis Rivers, as well as part of the Spray, were excluded. The area was reduced to 2,585 square miles. Yoho National Park area became 507 square miles and Glacier National Park 521 square miles. In 1949, the hydro-electric development on the Spray River resulted in the excision of the upper Spray Valley from Banff National Park. The same Act decreed that in the future all federal parks would be called 'National Parks of Canada,' and Rocky Mountains Park was re-named 'Banff National Park'. The Act stated that 'National Parks are dedicated to the Canadian people for their benefit, education and enjoyment, but they must be left unimpaired for the pleasure of future generations.'

Originally, the North West Mounted Police were responsible for keeping law and order and helping with fire and game control in the park area; however, in 1917, the Federal Government decided to turn parks policing over to provincial authority, and the Alberta Department of Police were to administer civil and criminal law. The move proved both unpopular and inadequate. The Royal North West Mounted Police were brought back the next year, and through them, the Federal Government continued to enforce provincial law. If any question of authority arose the Provincial Government would have to take steps to invest the Royal North West Mounted Police with the authority.[1]

In 1890, George Stewart had been appointed Justice of Peace for the park, and the North West Mounted Police were also authorized to try offenders. The residents objected. They said a park official would be biased, and the police should not prosecute and try the same case. They wanted an independent stipendiary magistrate. It was not until 1923, and the appointment of a stipendiary magistrate by the Provincial Government to be paid by the Federal Government that the question was settled. In 1930, the Parks Act provided for one or more stipendiary magistrates who would have exclusive jurisdiction with provincial laws. The Governor-General-in-Council might appoint a park resident as Justice of Peace for the purpose of the Act.

---

[1]From 1873 to 1904, the force was known as 'North West Mounted Police'; 1904 to 1920, as 'Royal North West Mounted Police'. In 1920, the name was changed to 'Royal Canadian Mounted Police'.

XII

The Park
and Industry

Banff, by 1911, had roads and trails built with attention to the many scenic views. Tally-hos were the favourite vehicles for sightseeing, no risky driving was allowed and all bridges had signs 'Walk the Horses'. Rustic pavilions and benches were scattered along footpaths and trails at strategic sites.

In 1907, land use for coal mining became an issue, which resulted in stricter regulations: a lease for twenty-one years at one dollar per acre, and an area limit of 2,560 acres; a royalty of five cents per ton and an output limit of ten tons per acre per year. If surface rights were wanted, they were sold at ten dollars per acre. Settlers could buy coal at the mouth of the mine and haul it themselves. The next year, fire and timber protection was required within the limit. In 1909, leases were extended to forty-two years and made renewable. In 1910, royalties increased to ten cents per ton; and, after disputes, were lowered to seven cents. By 1918, surface rights were not sold, only leased, at one dollar per acre, and all seams had to be approved before working.

Georgetown was a mining community which started in 1916. The Georgetown Coal Company operated on Rundle Mountain on the south side of the Bow River, about three miles west of Canmore. The company town had one store and a school, as well as houses for the miners. Finally they sold out to the Canmore Coal Company, and the buildings were all moved to Canmore.

Six years after the closing of the Bankhead mine, a briquette plant was opened in Canmore in 1929. Canmore had grown to a sizeable town with stores, houses and churches. Unfortunately, this development was halted by the great economic depression of the nineteen thirties. The output of briquettes was halved, and this, of course, led to unemployment and hardship; however, by 1930, Canmore was no longer in the Park, and earlier plans to make it a model mining town came to an end.

A silver mine was started at Eldon in 1915 across the valley from the old Silver City, but the First World War, 1914-18, ended the project, and no more mining was permitted in the park. Quartz mining was stopped by government order in 1916. Bill Peyto had previously filed on a talc mine in the Red Earth Creek area, but the government would not allow him to proceed. In 1921, he sold it to the National Talc Company, which put up cabins; it, too, was prohibited from bringing out talc. Not until the Second World War was there a relaxing of these restrictions. At that time talc was needed for insulation in electrical equipment, and a limited amount of talc was taken out.

Norman K. Luxton had a talc claim also, located north of Marble Canyon on the west side of the creek. Some talc was taken out of this mine, but when Luxton sold the mine to the National Talc Company, they did not develop it commercially, possibly owing to the difficulty with the Peyto mine. The talc, though fine in both claims, was not of the grade of French talc used for cosmetics.

In 1905, the Western Canada Cement and Coal Company, backed by the Canadian Pacific Railway, opened a plant at Exshaw. Two hundred acres were leased, at twenty-five cents per acre, for limestone quarrying to make cement, with a royalty of five percent on the gross output of usable rock. It was closed in 1916, only to be re-opened and worked twenty-four hours daily. The Parks Act of 1930, took Exshaw out of the park.

As early as 1889, the government made an effort to take lumbering out of the park by offering berths outside the parks in exchange. The Eau Claire gave up two, but kept the Spray berth. 1902 brought a park boundary extension, and timber berths were limited to 360 square miles at five dollars per square mile. Some of these belonged to the Canadian Pacific Railway. The Dominion Forestry Reserve Act of 1906 stated that no timber could be cut on the east slopes of the Front Range to protect water resources for ranchers and farmers on the plains. In 1906, yearly permits could be obtained for dry and dead timber at twenty-five cents per year. Mine props, posts, rails and cordwood could be taken free by the user. In 1915, a three-year permit for thirty square miles was given to thin out green timber and to cut timber where roads were to be constructed. When the Banff-Windermere highway was being built, three companies did this. They had portable saws at Castle Mountain where they cut props, saw logs and cordwood to ship to Calgary.

The Calgary Power Company applied for a development right to the Spray Valley in 1922. The Spray had been burned and timbered, and, possibly, the government might have given permission. William Pearce, a conservationist, said it would be a fire protection. However, public opinion made itself felt. By 1923, the Canadian National Parks Association had formed and fought the issue. Then the Provincial Government wanted to use the Spray for water storage, which produced more dissension. In 1930, the Spray was removed from the park, and more trouble resulted; because the depression was causing less work, the question of employment entered the argument. The Federal Government then shelved the whole problem, including Calgary Power's request. Nothing was resolved until 1948 when a hydro-electric development became a necessity.

An intensive survey was begun in May 1948, and road building started in September. Construction began in December and was well under way by January 1949. In 1951, the Spray Development, including the Three Sisters Plant, with a capacity of 3,000 kwh, the Spray Plant of 49,900 kwh and the Rundle Plant of 17,000 kwh, was completed and came into operation. In 1961, an extension to the Spray Development was completed, doubling the Plant capacity to 102,800 kwh. At the same time, a second unit was added to the Rundle Plant, increasing its capacity to 49,900 kwh.

The park had little hay land, but the increase of tourism increased the demand for horses. Also, the dairies in Banff needed grazing land for the cows. In 1914, owners of horses and cows paid one dollar per head per season and the government used the necessary marsh hay for the animal paddock and sold the rest to them. Both marsh hay and other hay could be cut only by tender, with the highest bidder doing the cutting.

Wild game had been plentiful on the eastern slopes of the Rockies, but the coming of settlement had decreased some species greatly. In 1890, the government had decreed there would be no hunting in the park, except for cougars, bears, wolves, lynx, wolverines, coyotes and hawks which were then regarded as predators; Banff could still outfit for hunting parties going outside the park. Until that year, there had been a temporary ranger, and when he died, the North West Mounted Police took his place. W.A. (Bill) Brewster was appointed as the first warden in 1901, but the area was too large for one man to cover. When the park came under the Forestry Branch in 1909, three forest and game wardens were appointed to enforce regulations and watch for fires. The first permanent warden, Howard Sibbald, was appointed as Chief Fire and Game Warden that year. In 1916, he had the very wide fire guard hand-cut on Sulphur Mountain; today new growth marks it clearly. By 1911, the National Parks Branch was anxious for a larger warden service, so there was an increase in the appropriation. J.B. Harkin increased the number of wardens; they cut trails, established caches and lookouts and built temporary shelters. Frank Dombert was in charge of the trail crews which, at that time, could number up to ten men. The Forestry Telephone was instituted. The wardens had instruction in fire fighting and the use of the portable gas pump in 1915. This was a light twin portable pumper of twenty-five pounds, fitted to an aluminum carrier which could be easily carried on the back, to which a two and a half inch hose could be connected. A properly proportioned oil and gas mixture was the fuel. These were used by the wardens along with the relay tanks, which were really nine foot, canvas containers. The water was pumped

Outing at Lake Minnewanka, circa 1906. Left to right: Dora Wilson, Ada Wilson, May McDougall, Bessie Wilson.

from the source to the first tank, if the fire was some distance away, and from that tank to the next and so on until the fire was reached. One of the Bow Summit fires was put out by this method, as were many others. By 1925, the wardens had five old Model T Ford cars for patrol, one Vickle fire truck, one Peterborough canoe on Lake Minnewanka, one worn out wooden boat, one worn out motor boat, and a Fairbanks-Morse speeder and a hand speeder, both in good condition, for railroad patrol. They also had a Barton front-end pumper which worked off the drive shaft of the truck. To this pump, on the front of the truck, a one and a quarter inch forestry hose could be attached, from which fire lines were fed.

In 1915, the Forestry Branch and the Parks Branch resorted to publicity to help prevent forest fires. All motorists entering the parks were given souvenir aluminium 'Buffalo Medicine' medals, in coloured paper folders, designed like Indian parfleche bags with Indian designs in colour, as well as car stickers reading 'Prevent Forest Fires'. The medal and parfleche idea was given to Mr. Harkin by N.K. Luxton when they were talking publicity.

In 1916, Canada and the United States agreed by treaty to protect migratory birds. The following year Parliament passed the Migratory Birds Convention Act and in 1918, regulations were established under it. Administration of these came to the Department of the Interior and to Commissioner Harkin. An ornithologist was appointed and the National

Parks Wildlife Division developed. Later, it was the Canadian Wildlife Service, and in 1966, it became a separate branch of the Department of Indian Affairs and Northern Development. In 1970, it was transferred to the Department of Fisheries and Forestry; today it is the Department of Environment, having been separated in 1971.

In 1916, Harkin also helped organize an interdepartmental Advisory Board of Wildlife Protection which functioned for nearly fifty years. That same year, cats were banned from the parks, and any dogs chasing game were destroyed, or the owners were sentenced to a fine of 500 dollars or three months in prison.

By 1930, there were decided increases in deer, moose, wapiti, goat, sheep and beaver. Bears had become troublesome, and some had to be destroyed. Bunting parties were allowed outside all park boundaries, where the overflow from the game preserves was sufficient for good sport.

The Canadian Forestry Association in 1924 suggested air patrol and radio telecommunications for fire protection in Banff and Kootenay Parks, but such surveillance was not established until many years later.

The Department of Marine and Fisheries established a Fish Hatchery in Banff in 1913 to raise fish for restocking lakes and rivers. There had been some government restocking before, by trying black bass in Lake Minnewanka and Nipigon trout in the Bow River; and the Canadian Pacific Railway had done some restocking. An auxiliary hatchery was established up the Spray, and later, a small one was installed in Jasper Park. In 1915, a fishing season was established, and a catch of only fifteen fish per day, none under seven inches, was the limit, and a licence had to be purchased. Five years later, the season was shortened even more.

William Whyte, Vice-President of the Canadian Pacific Railway, in 1904, presented the park with ten pheasants of eight different varieties, the nucleus of what was to become a famous aviary known worldwide. It was set up in the museum grounds. Three years later in the same grounds, a zoo was started. Enclosures, resembling the natural habitats of the animals, were constructed, and soon housed varieties of all the local bears, polar bears, mountain lions, lynx, raccoons, marmots, timber wolves, coyotes, wolverines and foxes. Both the aviary and the zoo interested the visitors. Unfortunately, in later years, the government did away with both, removing a real attraction from the town.

The first gift of three buffalo was from T.G. Blackstock, Q.C., of Toronto in 1897; then, in 1898, sixteen were given to the park by Lord Strathcona, who had a small number at *Silver Heights*, his estate in Winnipeg. They were temporarily housed at the old North West Mounted Police barracks, the log building serving as a shelter, and the grounds being strongly fenced. By June of 1898, the nineteen animals were enclosed on 300 acres, one and a half miles from Banff near Cascade Mountain, in a place visible from both the railway and the road to Lake Minnewanka, an advantage for visitors. By 1899, there were thirty buffalo, all doing well. Wapiti, moose, deer, Angora goats, Bighorn sheep, and in 1912, six yak, a gift from the Duke of Bedford, were added. In 1907, Howard Douglas went to Montana to bring the Pablo Buffalo Herd back to Canada.[1]

---

[1]See *Appendix* for a first-hand account of the amazing round-up.

XIII

Change in the Park

Banff townsite is still the 745 acres of the original survey and is mostly on the alluvial river terrace of the Bow, though over the years it has extended up the slopes of Tunnel and Sulphur Mountains. It is bounded on the north and south by Cascade and Sulphur Mountains and on the east by Tunnel Mountain. To the west are the drained swamps of the recreation grounds and Vermilion Lakes. Though the Bow River divides the town into north and south sections there are few riverside lots because of the high water table.

In the beginning, only Banff Avenue, Bear, Buffalo, Caribou and Lynx Streets were cleared for business and housing; then Beaver Street was opened for residents. The buildings were a typical frontier type, log and not large. The Brett Sanitorium and Moulton Park Hotel were the first hotels in the town. The first, a small building on the south side of the river, which gradually grew larger, was half hospital and half hotel; Moulton Park Hotel, situated where the picnic park is now, was built from logs of old buildings at Silver City, floated downstream on the Bow. A dance pavilion was built behind it in 1888 or 1889. Main Street, later Banff Avenue, was a combination of business and residences. One traveller wrote in 1892, "Two general stores, a chemist's shop, a baker, a bootmaker, blacksmith shop and a Chinese laundry occupy the chief street. Several churches and some houses and stores are dotted about in the village." By 1911, streets were open to Moose and in four more years to Fox, which opened the Badger area, and in 1917, the St. Julien section on Tunnel Mountain, though it was not until the 1940s and later that much building started there. Even by 1932, Spray and Cave Avenues south of the Bow had only thirty-two residences. Before cars came to Banff, it was a cold walk in winter across the bridge to the business section and the Post Office.

In 1904, the Banff Springs Hotel was being enlarged, and the Brett Sanitorium Hotel was three times the size of the original. The Alberta Hotel had been built and run by Frank Ricks and Williams Potts in 1901. When Potts left and went to Plattsburg, N.Y. in 1903, Ricks doubled the size of the

Mount Stephen House at Field, Yoho National Park.

hotel. In 1904, the King Edward Hotel, opened in 1903, was being enlarged. By 1911, the Banff Springs was adding another extension to their Tudor style frame building, and the Mount Royal Hotel had been built. In 1905, the Chateau Lake Louise had fifty rooms added.

The Canadian Pacific chalet at Field, 'Mount Stephen House', built at the same time as Glacier House, was enlarged. In 1905, a Superintendent's office was built in Field, and lots were open for lease by 1910. That year the government planted Balm-of-Gilead trees to make the streets attractive. Field was a divisional point for the railway, and most of the residents were Company employees. Mount Stephen House was closed in 1918, and only the Kicking Horse Tea House on the Big Hill was left to serve meals or tea to visitors in the 1920s.

By 1912, the government decided that construction in Banff was poor, so the following year a special permit had to be obtained for any alterations or any new building. It also commissioned T.H. Mawson, British architect and planner, to make proposals. He suggested recreation grounds, a circular drive around the west and northeast sides of Tunnel Mountain and a new site for the zoo to the north of the tracks. He also recommended that Banff Avenue be made level with the bridge and that the Middle Springs be developed.

In 1904, Dr. Brett had built an Opera House on the Sanitorium grounds, to be used for socials, plays and dances. The building was unusual because of its perfect acoustics.

In 1904 and 1905, lines were run from Bankhead for electricity. The Pacific Coal Company had agreed to the government's proposal to light Banff. Twelve arc lights were installed in strategic places on the streets; government buildings, public buildings, hotels and some residences had light. In 1911-1912, Calgary Power erected a small dam at the outlet of Lake Minnewanka for storage. The government had insisted on a thimble, a pipe with valves in the side of the dam for a water outlet, for future government power production. In 1924, the government authorized construction of a power house; and the thimble was utilized to supply all of Banff with electricity, because Bankhead was closing. Calgary Power took over the power supply for Banff in 1942 at the same rates as the government had charged.

Not until 1905-1906 were water mains and sewer lines laid in Banff; Forty Mile Creek was used as the source of water.

The house intended for Superintendent Stewart, situated on the banks of the Spray River, south of the Banff Springs Hotel, was not finished or used until the government needed a place for the first museum. This building was built on a rock slope, and a hole was blasted out of the rock to build the main floor. The second floor opened on to the upper ground level. This upper storey was finished for the museum, but as the location was not central enough, the government decided to move the top floor of the building. The new site was opposite the hospital on the corner of Spray Avenue and Mountain Drive. Everything was in place for opening in 1895. Most of the first natural history specimens came from the Department of Immigration. These specimens had been sent around Europe with other exhibits to show would-be-settlers what Canada was like. Mr. McLeod was the meteorologist and curator until his death, then Norman Sanson took over in 1896.

The government decided the Moulton Park Hotel and Dance Pavilion must come down to make way for a new museum building on Banff Avenue because the old one was too small. The new building was opened in 1903, and had room for natural history specimens, geological and botanical specimens, as well as a reading room with a library and park pamphlets. The government offices, including the superintendent's, moved there, as well as the telephone exchange. In 1896, Professor John Macoun had added to the botanical specimens and had done some cataloguing. He also left an interesting report on wild flowers in the park. A valuable Macoun collection of the flowers of the Selkirk Mountains was on display at Glacier House.

Norman B. Sanson, a native of Toronto, fought in the North West Rebellion of 1885 with the Queen's Own Rifles and came to Banff in 1892. His first work was as a bookkeeper for Dr. Brett and some town businesses. Sanson, as curator of the museum, was not only learned but intelligent and he loved his work. He walked and climbed thousands of miles looking for specimens for the museum and spent thousands of hours pressing flower specimens, and cataloguing them and geological specimens. He collected Indian artifacts as a personal hobby and presented this collection to Norman Luxton for the Luxton Museum, on the condition it was to remain there permanently as a separate complete collection, which it did until Luxton died. Sanson was a member of the Alpine Club of Canada from 1913 and became the first President of the Sky Line Hikers in 1933, retaining the office for three years.

In winter and in summer, Sanson climbed Sulphur Mountain weekly to check equipment and change record blanks. Through heavy winter snow on snowshoes, in rain and electrical storms, in blazing sun, he went. In 1931, the Rotarians had a sunrise breakfast on top of Sulphur Mountain in honour of his thousandth climb to the observatory, when they presented him with a medal and the freedom of the mountains. In 1948, the Geographic Board of Canada honoured him by naming the peak of the Sulphur Range on which the observatory stood 'Sanson Peak'. Probably his last climb up there was in 1945 when he went to make observations on the eclipse of the sun; he was then eighty-three years of age.

Norman Sanson was tall, lean, and always wore English tweeds. He read much and could quote poetry freely. He built a very modern air-conditioned house but would not live in it, preferring his old type bachelor home. He could be taciturn, but he could also be very droll, and though he had a reputation of being a man of few words, the writer can testify that he was an interesting raconteur.

A bridle-trail was started to the top of Sulphur Mountain in 1902, and both it and an observatory were finished the next year. The observatory was a stone building 14 feet x 15 feet, with an observation tower 26 feet high. This was built at a point, 8,756 feet above sea level, later called Sanson Peak. Here wind velocity and currents, as well as temperature, were automatically recorded. A seven-strand wire cable connected it to the museum in town.

The Alpine Club of Canada, founded by Sir Sandford Fleming, Dr. Grant and Major Rogers on the memorable occasion when they had reached the summit of Rogers Pass, had disappeared into oblivion. In 1901, Arthur O. Wheeler, who was doing photo-topographical surveys in the Selkirks, went to Glacier House to get information about mountain climbing and met Professor Charles E. Fay of the Appalachian Club. The two men discussed an Alpine Club of Canada. Wheeler's idea was received with indifference until he met the Reverend Doctor J.C. Herdman, pastor of the Presbyterian Church in Calgary, who was an enthusiastic mountain climber. In 1902, Professor Fay's suggestion of a Canadian Alpine Club as a branch of the American Club was met with extreme indignation from Mrs. H.J. Parker, a staff writer of the *Winnipeg Free Press*. J.W. Dafoe offered his paper's columns

The 1000th ascent of Sulphur Mountain by N.B. Sanson (front left).

for Alpine Club propaganda and Doctor Herdman persuaded the *Calgary Herald* to do the same. The result of this publicity was that Mr. Marpole, General Superintendent of the Western Division of the Canadian Pacific Railway, Mrs. J.W. Henshaw, botanist, the Very Reverend Dean Paget and Dr. A.P. Coleman, geologist, were interested. Through Mr. Marpole, Mr. Wheeler met Mr. William Whyte (later Sir William), second Vice-President of the Canadian Pacific Railway. Whyte granted Wheeler twenty passes for return fare to Winnipeg from anywhere on the railroad to bring delegates to Winnipeg for a conference.

March 27th and 28th, 1906 were the dates set for the meeting. Mrs. Parker persuaded the Young Men's Christian Association to offer accommodation, arranged for Mr. Wheeler to be guest speaker at the Canadian Club luncheon and for Doctor Herdman to lecture and show slides the evening of the 27th.

On the afternoon of the 28th the constitution was drawn up and election of officers took place. Sir Sandford Fleming was Honorary President, A.O. Wheeler, President, Dr. A.P. Coleman and Reverend J.C. Herdman, Vice-Presidents, Mrs. H.J. Parker, Secretary. The first annual camp was to be at

Peyto Lake, July 9th to 16th. The yearly subscription was twenty-five dollars and an Alpine Journal was to be published when funds allowed. The Canadian Pacific Railway, Royal North West Mounted Police and park authorities loaned flies and tents and the outfitters of Banff, Field and Glacier sent free guides and horses to help with the first camp. Actually, the first camp of the Alpine Club of Canada was at Summit Lake on the pass connecting Emerald Lake Valley to the Yoho Valley.

By 1907 there were 201 members, the first issue of the *Canadian Alpine Journal* was published, and the club had become international.

In 1909, the government gave the Alpine Club of Canada a building site midway between Banff and the Upper Hot Springs. The Club House was finished by 1910, with a lounge, dining hall and a very fine library. Tent cabins were erected to house climbers. It was a delightful place, and much used by all climbers. Because the Alpine Club brought so many visitors, the government, in 1914, gave them a thousand dollar grant to help the good publicity. In 1920, A.O. Wheeler started organized walking tours which were less expensive than climbs requiring horses to reach the mountains. These tours were Wheeler's own private venture and caused controversy with the Alpine Club members who felt Wheeler was using the Club to further his own ends. Credit, however, must go to Arthur O. Wheeler for his efforts in encouraging mountaineering in the Banff area. In 1973, the Club built a new Club House in Canmore, although the old one stood on Sulphur Mountain until 1974, scene of many happy memories.

More visitors and larger appropriations were the cause of the opening of more lots in 1914 and the tightening of building regulations. The following year, buildings had to be better, and all plans authorized by Ottawa. This led to the development of a technical division headed by an engineer, and in 1921, the town planning office was transferred to the National Parks Branch from the Conservation Commission. Harkin was insistent that the town should have a better appearance and that the comfort of visitors should be considered. During the 1930s, efforts were made to make Banff a year-round resort. There was an annual clean-up day for the town; a fine was set for spitting on the streets. False fronts were put on many business buildings on Banff Avenue, and others were replaced. On Arbor Day, the school children planted trees in appropriate places and made flower gardens in the school grounds.

In 1915, the government drained a large swamp on the south side of the Bow River to form the recreation grounds. They secured the services of the famous architect Frank Lloyd Wright assisted by F.C. Sullivan, to build a pavilion. This building was fitted with stoves as well as large fireplaces, and a plentiful supply of firewood. Benches and long tables were in the big room. Here people could come and cook meals and be comfortable on a wet day. There were many day-excursions by train from Calgary, and organizations also came for a day in the mountains. The building was well used by thousands. In the grounds, the government laid out tennis courts and had swings, slides, merry-go-rounds and see-saws for the children. The pavilion was used until finally it was demolished after the Second World War. It was replaced by cooking shelters with tables, benches and barbecue pits.

In 1923, the government started work on the present bridge. The old one was moved down stream for use during construction. The sculptor, Mr. Thompson, from Calgary, carved the Indian heads which one sees on the sides.

The houses moved from Bankhead were used to provide extra residences and summer cottages, the renting of the latter having become good business in Banff. The citizens had developed by free enterprise many amusements for the tourist. From 1888, J. Ryan had provided canoes and then a launch, the *Mountain Belle*, on the Bow River. By 1904, the boathouse, which had been taken over by William Mather from W. Roper in the late 1890s, was ready with a new motor launch to replace the old *Mountain Belle*, and more canoes and rowboats were provided. On Banff Avenue, there was a pool hall, and more stores opened with souvenirs, furs, Indian crafts and game heads. Tea rooms and restaurants took care of the hungry visitor. By 1929, there were eight hotels and many private rooming houses, cabin-shacks and tent-houses. The last two were discouraged by the government after 1938. As car travel increased, bungalow camps developed in the town, and in the next forty years motels were built. Many of these business enterprises were open only during the summer months.

In 1925, when it was being opened for the summer, the Chalet burned down at Lake Louise. The Canadian Pacific built the present Chateau and opened it the following year. Before cars came into the park, the Company ran the *Lake Louise Tramway*, an electric trolley on a track, from the station to the Chateau. If people wanted to drive the two and a half miles in a tally-ho, their luggage went in the trolley. After automobiles arrived, the track was taken out; parts of the old track bed, now grass covered, are still visible from the road.

In 1926, the Banff Springs lost its north wing to fire, but carried on business in the centre block and south wing. The Company had been replacing the old Tudor building by sections; the centre block, built of Rundle Stone, was finished before the fire, so in 1926-27 they erected the north wing, and had it ready for business the next spring. In 1927-1928, they built the south wing which completed the hotel as it is today. Mr. Michael Delahanty, who had worked in resort hotels for the Canadian Pacific, was given the task of choosing furnishings and becoming manager of the new Banff Springs. Mr. Delahanty was a clever decorator and took a real interest; every chair, cabinet, table and lounge was designed for a specific place. The large bedroom suites were named 'Swiss', 'The Tudor', 'The Scandinavian', and so on, and

The Banff Springs Hotel, circa 1890.

all were fitted out with the proper period fixtures and furnishings. The Royal suites had dining room, lounges, reception room, kitchen and bedrooms for royalty and their immediate retinue. The ballroom was illuminated by hidden lighting and had a conservatory off the north end which was kept delightful with exotic plants. The whole atmosphere of the hotel was one of quiet, dignified elegance. Tea in the Riverview Lounge was graciously served. The Alhambra dining room, with Spanish decor, and the Fairholme dining room offered excellent cuisine and service in charming surroundings. Guests indulged in sports during the day and, in the evening, dressed formally for dinner and dancing. That was an age when people lived graciously, travelled leisurely and still had courtesy. Today from the outside the building is just as beautiful, but inside there is only a feeling of commercialism and hurry.

When the first Grand View Villa Hotel owned by Dr. Brett burned in 1901, the government decided to manage the Hot Springs. The new bath house was 40 feet x 40 feet and divided into two parts, each of which had four private tubs, a steam room, a cooling room and hot and cold showers. There were also two inside plunges. The outside pool had dressing rooms on each side. The pool was 48 feet x 24 feet and was adjacent to the bath house where one got a towel and a respectable bathing costume: skirts, sleeves and all for the ladies, sleeves and knee-length suits for the gentlemen, all for twenty-five cents, including the swim. A caretaker's house was built across the garden by the building. Eight more tub baths were added the following year. That old pool, open to the sky but surrounded by the building, was a picture in the winter when hoar frost curtains hung three 1 to four feet long around it.

In 1904, a new pool 100 feet x 50 feet with a depth four to nine feet was built at the Cave and Basin, an addition was made to the bath house and a wood-burning furnace added to heat it. The laundry was adjacent and it did washing for both the Upper Hot Springs and the Basin.

The second caretaker of the Cave and Basin was David Drummond Galletly, who came to Banff in 1886; and he was connected with the Cave and Basin for twenty years. He was caretaker-manager during a Liberal administration, and when the Conservatives came into power, he became the visitor's guide for the Cave. He always wore his tartan and his Scottish tarn o'shanter which, along with his friendly, kind and courteous manner, delighted the visitors. He always said, "Happiness is the only good. The place to be happy is here. The time to be happy is now. The way to be happy is to make others happy." Well, he certainly made many visitors happy with his stories told in the cave.

In 1911, the government brought in Walter Painter, an architect, who designed the present Cave and Basin, which was constructed in 1912-1914. Mr. Walter Painter had come originally from Redding, Pennsylvania to Montreal where the Canadian Pacific had employed him to study the Chateau-type hotels. He designed part of the Chateau Frontenac in Quebec City and did the centre block of the Banff Springs, as well as the old Hotel Vancouver and part of the Empress in Victoria. He finally made his permanent home in Banff.

In the early days, many crutches were nailed to the trees along the path to the Cave and Basin; and at the Upper Hot Springs, the handrails along the hundred or more steps to the Grand View Villa were reinforced with crutches. These were the mute testimony of the many hundreds of people who came unable to walk, and left so much better. Dr. Brett, in 1913, obtained permission to bottle water from the Kidney Springs, just a short distance down the road from the Upper Hot Springs. This he sold to visitors. Exploitation to the fullest!

In the beginning, the government viewed Minnewanka as a possible summer resort. Villa lots were laid out by the government, and a chalet, the Beach House was built by Walter Astley. This chalet became well known for Mrs. Charles Astley's fish dinners and afternoon teas after she and her husband Charles took it over from his brother. In 1899, the Canadian Pacific put a new launch on the lake and built a pier 200 feet long. There was another chalet built on the south shore in the early 1900s, owned and run by Norman Luxton, who also operated a cruise ship. When the lake was to be raised the first time, he had a big dinner for most of the Banff people at the end of which the chalet was set on fire by him. They watched as the flames cast weird and awesome reflections on the lake. He built a second chalet on the north shore, but at the second raising of the lake, he gave it all up, and sold the chalet and his cruiser.

In 1912, when Calgary Power built the storage dam, the lake was raised. The original settlement was moved to higher ground on a large peninsula between Cascade Bay and the main lake. Most of these remained until the second raising of the lake in 1941. The majority of the lots were leased by Calgarians, about fifteen in number. One of the chalets was moved to higher ground and operated by Captain Standly, who ran his steamship, the *Daughter of the Peaks*. Captain Jack Standly was a real character. He delighted in playing to an audience and in shocking people. One of his favourite pastimes was to don a striped red and white knee-length bathing suit with sleeves and mount his bicycle just before the time for a launch trip. He would peddle furiously, sail down the ramp to the wharf, make feeble efforts to slow the bicycle and go off the wharf end into the lake. Gasps, screams and consternation from the visitors! Finally, Jack would bob up, towing his bike – and, of course, willing hands helped him out of the water. He, with a beaming smile, graciously thanked all and walked away. Jack was a great story teller, but Len Smith, who later took over the launch, was even better at 'tall tales'.

In 1923, the government started construction on the power house in Devil's Canyon to make use of the water in the lake. Three houses were built near the dam on Cascade Bay for the superintendent, Major Enoch Smith, and for his operators. One Christmas Eve day, the whole country was snowed in, and the people at Minnewanka were isolated. No going to Banff for either goodies or mail. Suddenly, out of nowhere, came a jingle of bells, dogs barking and there was good old Ike Mills with his dog-team and sleigh. Santa had arrived – so had the turkey – and all was saved.

Ike Mills was probably one of the best-known men in Banff and belonged to the group who found Banff the treasure at the rainbow's end. Some others of that good company were Jim Simpson, Walter Peyto, Ben Woodworth, Senior, Mary Schaffer Warren, George Paris, Colonel Philip Moore, Dave White, Byron Harmon, Dr. Bert Ashton and Norman Luxton. All these people found something in Banff that sustained them in their many ambitions and frustrations until they died.

Ike, as he was known, came in 1910 from Yorkshire, England. For some years he drove the four-horse team on the tally-ho to pick up visitors at the station to take them to the Banff Springs Hotel. He then started the Mills Riding School, and from that, came the Mills Stables where he rented horses to visitors.

The Daughter of the Peaks *on Lake Minnewanka.*

In the winter, he had his Husky dog-team. In the 1920s, Calgary to Banff dog-team racing was popular, and often Ike was a winner. In 1926 and 1928, he was one of the winners in the Strongheart Trophy dog race. Ike made trips to Sunshine, Skoki and Assiniboine; and legend has it that he transported the first stove into Skoki Lodge by dog sled. Mail and visitors were taken to out-of-the-way places by Ike and his dogs.

He married Alma La Palme in May of 1938 in Boston, when he was returning from a trip to the Old Country. Mrs. Mills did not arrive in Banff until the end of June because she had music and radio commitments. She was not a stranger as she had played the cello in the concert orchestra at the Banff Springs Hotel in the 1920s.

Late in 1940, construction started on the present dam, slightly down stream from the old one. That was the end of Devil's Canyon, which is now a beauty spot for the fish under the lake waters. The chalet and summer cottages had been torn down and the three government houses moved to Banff before the lake was raised.

Today there is a small confectionery store, and there are launches, and rowboats for the fishermen. Skin divers try to explore Lake Minnewanka, but the lake is very deep, so much remains obscure. The old Devil's Lake, the scene of early explorers, Indian and white hunters, and backdrop for movies, is greatly changed. Gone are favourite bays and camping spots – but – the 'Big Ones' are still caught, as any fisherman will tell you.

The first Post Office in Banff townsite was in a small building on the east side of Banff Avenue, and Dick O'Donahue was the first postmaster. When he resigned, L. Fulmer became postmaster, with A.N. Saddington his assistant. Fulmer combined his store, residence and post office in a building where the King Edward Hotel is now. He left Banff in 1900; and the mail was taken over by George and William Fear, and run by Arthur N. Saddington, postmaster, in the Fear store. Mails increased as the town grew, so the Post Office moved into the building next door (about where the Garbert Building is). There A.N. Saddington and his staff worked for many years. When the Administration Building was finished in 1936, they moved into the east end of it. Very soon the space was needed, and in 1956, the Post Office Building was built on the corner of Buffalo and Bear Streets where it is today. The Post Office is always one of the busiest places in town because visitors in all seasons mail many post cards, and philatelists want stamps for collections.

The history of the churches in Banff is comparable to that of any small town in the Canadian west. The Roman Catholic and Methodist came first, followed by the Anglican and Presbyterian. For twelve years the Presbyterians and Methodists shared the Presbyterian Church on Bear Street and alternated ministers. Then, when the denominations united, the continuing Presbyterians built their church on the corner of Banff Avenue and Wolf Street; and Rundle United, on the corner of Banff Avenue and Buffalo Street, finally replaced the old Methodist wooden church which had faced Banff Avenue. The Anglicans had services in the town hall until they could build 'St. George's in The Pines' on the corner of Beaver and Buffalo Streets. In the early days, it was known as the English Church. The foundation stone was laid in 1889, by Lord Stanley, Governor-General of Canada, and the chancel, built in 1897, first had canvas walls so that it could be used until the church was completed. The carillon of bells was a gift of Dr. Brett and was dedicated by Bishop Pinkham of Calgary in 1927. They are similar to those in the Peace Tower in Ottawa but smaller. In 1926, the Brewster family gave the Westminster Chimes clock in memory of their parents.

The Roman Catholic Church moved from its old site (where the Scout Hall is) to the corner of Lynx and Squirrel Streets. Their stone church has most interesting stained glass windows which, behind the Biblical scenes, show mountains and views of Banff. They were specially made at the request of Father McGuinness, who was the architect for the church. Today Banff has several other attractive churches, representative of other denominations.

Banff never had the traditional 'little red school house'. First of all, school was taught in a tent on Bear Street, then in a small log building on the same street near the corner of Caribou. In 1892, a school was built on Banff

The Wilson & Fear store with proprietors Will Fear (left) and Tom Wilson, 1895.

Avenue next to the old school Auditorium which is the Information Bureau today. That school became too crowded, and in 1913, a brick and cobblestone school was built on the grounds where the Composite High School is now, but to the south of it, closer to Wolf Street. The next was a primary school where Composite High is today; and the old school became the High School. Finally, the old schools were replaced by the present ones. In earlier days, the school grounds had many fine large spruce trees, as well as a playground, lawns and garden. The old brick school had a peaked roof and gables which suited the mountain scenery much better than the modern 'packing case' architecture of the present school.

The first school on Banff Avenue became the fire hall in the days when horses were used. Part of it was used for government offices and the telephone office when both were moved from the museum building. When the old fire hall was tom down, the fire hall was moved into the government building at the corner of Beaver and Caribou Streets where it is today, and the telephone office moved to the new Telephone Building on Beaver Street. Banff has a fire chief and a voluntary fire brigade who have fought fires that have threatened whole sections of town. The government has had the responsibility of keeping the hydrants open in the winter, when temperatures drop below freezing.

Banff, like all towns, has had many fires in homes, livery barns, and business places. In February, 1914, on a morning when it was twenty-six degrees below zero, the King Edward Block burned in the most spectacular and destructive fire up to that time. The hotel, the Lux Theatre, the King Edward bar, J.D. Anderson's Tailor Shop, Carl Friesen's Electric Shop, King Edward Tour office and the sample room for commercial travellers all burned. Only the brick projection room for the theatre was left standing, and it was completely gutted. The Brewster Trading Co., next to the theatre, was saved with difficulty, and the Mount Royal Hotel across the street was blistered by heat. The whole street was endangered. Because of the very heavy timbers used in the construction of the block, it burned slowly, and the contents of the stores and bar and some of the furnishings of the hotel were saved. All the hotel guests rescued their possessions, and the Brewster Trading Co. got their stock out in the event that building burned also.

The fire bell rang about 8 a.m. The volunteer brigade and citizens arrived. Then trouble, the hydrant by the King Edward was frozen solid, the one by the Mount Royal likewise. Half an hour had gone when the chemical engine arrived, and it would not start. In another half hour a trickle of water came from the Bear Street hydrant, but the hoses were frozen and useless. Hay and wood were piled around the hydrants and ignited to thaw them out. The police and government people had arrived, but another hour went by before water flowed. By then, all that could be done was to save the other buildings. The men at work at the Banff Springs Hotel came with hoses; Bankhead sent their brigade and hoses; Calgary phoned and said they would come.

By late afternoon, all was on the ground. The Brewster Trading Co. stock and the hotel furnishings were looted to the sum of 15,000 dollars while most people were fighting to save things, and the King Edward Block loss was 47,425 dollars.

A government inquiry was conducted by P.C. Barnard-Hervy, Chief Superintendent for Dominion Parks. The hearing revealed that the fire brigade had no quarters and that the hose was kept on reels on the street. Fire Chief Charles Stenton said 300 feet of hose was frozen, only the Bear Street hydrant was open with very low pressure, the chemical engine did not work because the domes were eaten through by the acid and the hose was ruined. Defective wiring had started the fire in a room above the tailoring shop, and Bill Furnell, who did all the electric wiring for Banff and Bankhead, was questioned. The inquiry also revealed the government officers had been negligent and that both they and the police were too slow in arriving at the fire. The best result for Banff was that the hydrants were never again left frozen. As soon as the inquiry ended, N.K. Luxton started to rebuild, and he called it the Lux Block which included the hotel, stores and theatre as today. But the hotel, today, is not as it was. It used to have a large rotunda with comfortable lounges and chairs, tables and writing desks, and a large fireplace

the original King Edward Hotel

to gather around. The big dining room was attractive, and the meals had much variety in wild game and wild fowl, as well as fish, local and imported. Christmas and New Year's dinners were long and leisurely. Not a luxury hotel like the Banff Springs, the King Edward could and did take its own place and the old hotel registers show many well known names.

In the dead of winter, in 1917, when the temperature was twenty-five below, the fire bell rang about 11:30 p.m. The fire brigade, citizens, government men and police were soon on the spot. In spite of all the water, nothing could save the Harmony Theatre built by Byron Harmon four years before. After a long struggle, the fire was controlled, but the next morning, great icicles mocked the burned and blackened facade.

The Mount Royal Hotel fire, in 1967 was a flaming holocaust which started near midnight. The Banff Fire Brigade and the citizens, as well as the Canmore Fire Brigade, government employees, the Gas Company and the Royal Canadian Mounted Police, did a marvellous work that night in saving the avenue. Citizens guarded roofs on the buildings from flying debris. The firemen's clothes soon caked with ice, and to carry on their work, they had to remove some garments; looters made away with four helmets, three coats and three pairs of knee-length boots. Human nature seems to change little. The stores saved their stock, but guests of the hotel were evacuated in their nightwear. Arthur Hailey was one of the guests, and he had the manuscript for his book *Airport* which he took with him. Gerda Christoffersen was another guest and took time to save her paintings.

The next morning, only the elevator shaft was left standing. One of the irreplaceable losses was a number of pictures by Mrs. Drummond Davis. The old landmark, built in 1907, by D. McDougall and Rattray, who sold out to McDougall the next year, had become well known to world travellers. McDougall changed the name from Banff Hotel to 'Mount Royal' and so it was when he sold it to James Brewster in 1912. When the Greyhound Company, who had bought it from Jim Brewster's family, rebuilt in 1968 after the fire, they kept the old name.

Banff had many hotels in its beginning, most of which have disappeared. This is shown clearly in Frank Beattie's experience. Frank Beattie ran one of the first hotels at the Upper Hot Springs, which he named Hot Springs Hotel and which stood about where the Rimrock Hotel is today. Next he had the Beattie House on Banff Avenue which he advertised as, "The only dollar a day house in Banff. Good rooms. Good meals. Good beds. Bar. American Plan." Then he took over the Park Hotel which had wide verandahs with several chairs, which were seldom vacant. In May, 1900, he advertised Lee House on Banff Avenue for rent, then sold it to George Allan an ex-North West Mounted Policeman. This was near the Paris Tearoom. Beattie then handled the mail for a time, and after that, went into the transfer business. Finally, he had a pool hall on Banff Avenue.

The Homestead Hotel was built in 1910 by John Locke in the same place the new building stands now. It was enlarged then sold to D.M. Soole and A.W. Faulkner in 1919. Then it was enlarged more, and Soole, after a trip to England in the 1920s, built the separate inn-like dining room, which still stands. This part was not demolished when the main hotel was replaced in 1974. In 1934 Soole commissioned Charles Beil to model the storks for the hotel as an omen of good luck. Finally, in 1945, Earle Gammon and James McLeod bought the Homestead, and eventually Gammon took it over. Hotels came into existence and disappeared, today leaving only four of the earlier ones. The 'Alberta' became the 'Cascade', but the Mount Royal, King Edward and Homestead kept their original names, if not their original buildings.

The first hotels had many stories told about them. One that comes down to us is that one of the early hotels used to sell drinks on the quiet on Sunday. When a very tall man came in on a Sunday, the bartender looked him over carefully and said, "Hello, Shorty, what are you going to have?" The tall stranger as it turned out was F. Langford, the licence inspector, and it was a long, long time before any more Sunday drinks were served in that particular hotel.

An ex-railroad conductor asked the first inhabitants of Banff if they would like a newspaper and if so, would they be willing to subscribe to

Hotel Bretton Hall

expenses. The idea was well received, so the first issue of the *Hot Springs Record* came out June 21, 1887 Vol. 1 No. 1 – then the editor absconded with the funds. In April 1888, C.B. Halpin (later with the *Lacombe Globe*) published *National Park Life*. Halpin had many ups and downs ending in an up in less than a year when his press went up in smoke. John Innis, the well-known artist, tried to revive the *National Park Life,* but it was hard going, and the paper died after a number of issues. In April, 1893, W. Hanson Bourne started the *Rocky Mountain Echo,* but it, too, failed. Ike Byers, in 1900, started the *National Park Gazette* and published it until September, 1901. Dr. Whyte, Dr. Brett's partner, bought the press, and on December 25th, Dr. Brett brought out his famous 'Convention Issue.' Then there were no newspapers until April, 1902, when Norman Luxton started the *Crag and Canyon.* He bought the old water-power press from Dr. Brett and continued to own the paper and issue it until 1958, when he sold it. His first three editors were Dick Burd, W.H. Kidner and W.P. Stanley. Luxton always reserved as his prerogative that he could write editorials or articles as long as he owned the paper. The *Crag and Canyon* is still being published though it has changed hands since Luxton sold it. During the first war, the Brewsters ran the *Rocky Mountain Courier* for three or four years in opposition. Apparently there was some feud, political or otherwise, between the Brewsters and Luxton at the time. Then the feud ended, and so did the *Courier.*

As early as 1903, Howard Douglas had tried to convince the government that the motor car was here to stay. Despite this information, in 1905, an Order in Council forbade all cars entry to the park. The question had been reviewed and the results arrived at were that roads were not suitable, local liveries and hotels were against it, William Pearce said horses and cars did not go together, and riders on horseback would be endangered. By 1909, the Calgary-Banff highway was being built, the Provincial Government having started it in 1907; in the same year, despite government regulations, the Calgary Auto Club invaded Banff and drove all around the town. By 1911, the road was finished and it was possible to travel to Banff. The Federal Government finally bowed to the inevitable and allowed cars to be brought into the town. They were restricted to the main roads to the hotels, could only be driven at fifteen miles an hour, and eight miles an hour in the townsite. In the very beginning, visitors had to leave their cars at the police barracks next to the museum on Banff Avenue. After 1912, each car owner paid a dollar per trip, or five for the season, and had to be registered. By 1918, the speeds had risen to thirty miles per hour with twenty miles per hour in the townsite. The trouble with all existing roads was that they had to be made usable for cars. In Banff, for instance, on Tunnel Mountain Drive, the corkscrew had to be eliminated. This section, which had thrilled many a visitor in a tally-ho, was useless for a car. Though there were many taxi-drivers, the first woman taxi-driver in Banff was not to appear until 1919, when Mrs. H.M. Heath drove a sightseeing limousine for the Y.W.C.A. Hotel. Harriet Mary Parkinson Heath, originally from Roland, Manitoba, came to Claresholm as a school teacher. She contracted tuberculosis and was sent to Banff where the dry air was believed to have certain therapeutic value. She remained in Banff and began driving ill and wounded veterans who had been sent to the hospital for treatment. She was known to them as "Aunt Molly", a term of endearment.

As early as 1904-05, work on Yoho Park roads was proceeding. The road up Yoho Valley into Takkakaw Falls followed the old Monarch Mine pack trail. The major difficulty to overcome on the Yoho road was the switchback section, where even today a bus has to stop and back up before continuing up the canyon.

J.B. Harkin repeatedly said, as Douglas had before him, that roads were the essential link between the parks and the world. More appropriations were set aside for road construction. In August, 1914, the Great War started, and enemy aliens, who were sent to the internment camp at Castle, were put to work on the Banff-Lake Louise and Banff-Vermilion Pass roads, west of Castle. In the winter, the internees cut trees from road allowances or cleared brush until the snow became too deep; then they were moved to the camp opposite the Cave and Basin, and one pool (now gone) was set aside for their use. During the 1930s, in the depression years, the unemployed worked on roads, and the Banff-Jasper road was begun as a relief project – not to be finally finished until 1940, although an interim road was used before the completion of today's highway.

By 1921, all types of cars were coming to Banff, but it was not until 1927 that the last stretch from Lake Louise to Field and Golden was finished and cars were allowed into Yoho. This link was important, because a road had been built from Golden to Radium making a circle drive from Banff that the alert Canadian Pacific Railway was to call 'Lariat Drive'.

In 1916, the park section of the Banff-Windermere Highway was completed, but British Columbia had not finished its section. J.B. Harkin and Randolph Bruce, Lieutenant-Governor of British Columbia, met the British Columbia Government in 1919, and an agreement was made to complete the road. In the agreement, a strip five miles wide on each side of the highway was to become Kootenay National Park, which was created in 1920. The highway was formally opened June, 1923 at Kootenay Crossing where the Lieutenant-Governors of Alberta and British Columbia cut the ribbon. This memorable ceremony opened a 6,000-mile system of roads through Canada and the United States, connecting the California-Oregon Line and the Grand Canyon Route. It also gave access to twelve United States National Parks and three Canadian National Parks.

In 1881, Radium Hot Springs was owned by John McKay because it was on his homestead. Early in the 1900s, an English company bought the 615 acres, including the springs, and built a bath-house and a concrete pool, or reservoir, and charged fifty cents for anyone wanting to bathe. The Federal Government tried to negotiate the acquisition of this acreage, but the company refused. So, in 1919, an amendment to the Dominion Forest Reserve Act was passed permitting the government to expropriate any land necessary for park purposes. In 1922, the Federal Government expropriated the company's land, paying them 22,000 dollars compensation. An Order-in-Council the same year changed the park boundaries to exclude from the park as many settlers having crown grants as possible. Finally, in 1926, the area of Kootenay National Park was changed to 587 square miles.

Between 1916 and 1923 branch roads were built to Emerald Lake and Moraine Lake. In 1929, the Big Bend, the link to the Coast, by-passed Glacier and spelled its isolation until the Rogers Pass stretch became the last link in the Trans-Canada Highway in 1962. Now Glacier is once more accessible to the camper, climber and hiker.

XIV

Banff
and the Visitor

The development of the automobile had the effect, not only of increasing the number of travellers, but of changing the social nature of the travelling public. Tourism was no longer the prerogative of the wealthy elite as it had been at an earlier period. The new travellers were not people who demanded luxurious accommodation. Rather were they people who were satisfied with either a campsite or a not too expensive room. After a number of them began camping at the junction of Forty Mile Creek and the Bow, the government decided it would be better to open an official campground at the foot of Mount Rundle where the Spray flows into the Bow. This would reduce the fire hazard and litter. Rundle Mountain Camp was soon filled to overflowing with hundreds of tents of all colours, shapes and sizes.

In 1911, the Canadian Pacific Railway had built a nine hole golf course on the flats of the Bow. When the government took it over, an eighteen hole course was laid out, a special golf course architect being hired for the purpose. In the 1930s, the Canadian Pacific proposed to resume control of the golf course. They planned to build a club house and to alter the course. The Railway Company, therefore, made a deal with the government whereby the Company would provide the labour to move the campsite, which was scarcely an attractive sight to the guests at the Banff Springs Hotel. Drying laundry did not add to the beauty of the Loop Drive around the golf course.

The location of the new campsite was the terrace above and along King Edward VII Highway near the Hoodoos. This Tunnel Mountain Camp met with a lot of opposition from the citizens of Banff, mainly because it was too far from town and would not help business; nevertheless, the camp was moved. In 1926, the government passed regulations compelling campers to maintain a decent level of camping; the fee was one dollar for three weeks or four dollars for a season. Every person was warned about campfires and urged to put all litter in the proper containers provided.

In the years that followed, Tunnel Mountain Camp was extended many times. Shelters for meals, with tables and benches, shower and wash houses, toilets, garbage cans on each lot, sewage disposal and electric lights were added. Trailers needed more space and more facilities. Two Jack Lake and its overflow camp, on the road to Lake Minnewanka, added two more campgrounds. Now picnic parks and campsites have been established through all the parks.

With the opening up of the park for car travel, some far-seeing individual saw the potential of the area for other than leisurely pursuits. Where could the fine arts be better taught than in Banff; with its beautiful surroundings? So thought Dr. E.A. Corbett, head of the Department of Extension of the University of Alberta, who was responsible for extra-mural education in rural Alberta for nearly sixteen years. This man encouraged the arts in Alberta, and assisted by Elizabeth Sterling Haynes, a drama teacher, he encouraged local performers. From 1920 to 1935, small town dramatic clubs knew him, and appreciated his sense of humour and his democratic ideas.

In 1933, with a Carnegie grant of ten thousand dollars to the Department of Extension of the University of Alberta, Dr. Corbett started a school of the 'Arts Related to the Theatre' in Banff. Tenting and camping space were offered as accommodation. A garage was used as a dining hall; Banff Public and High Schools provided classrooms and the Bretton Hall Theatre (the old Opera House) was used during the early years. In 1935, Dr. Corbett went to Ottawa, and his assistant, Donald Cameron, took over.

This was in the depression years, but the School grew; scholarships were given when at all possible; fees ranged from one to five dollars. Donald Cameron used the town school for dormitories and had a convoy haul the beds from Edmonton. In 1936, the painting and piano divisions were added; later, singing, writing and French were also added.

In 1939, the old theatre was condemned, so the Banff School Board went to the people, who agreed to an increase in taxes to build the Auditorium (Information Office now) on Banff Avenue; it opened January, 1940. The Federal Government gave the School a perpetual lease, at a nominal tax rate, over a large area of land on Tunnel Mountain. On its present site since 1947, the Banff School of Fine Arts has never looked backwards.

Donald Cameron, a man of vision and strong convictions, developed an institution for the fine arts which became known world wide. Although practically a dictator of the school policy and management, he nevertheless gave his teaching staff full freedom to develop their courses as they chose. He brought in such people as A. Y. Jackson, Walter Phillips, and Annora Brown to teach art; Mrs. Sterling Haynes for drama, Gwyneth Lloyd for ballet; Jacques Jolas and Glyndwr Jones for music; and countless others for the various divisions. In the beginning, the Painting Division was A.C. Leighton's Painting School for Kananaskis, which later amalgamated with the School of Fine Arts. The policy has always been to emphasize creative teaching and production; the students have freedom to develop their own pictures, songs, plays and stories.

Now, with over ten thousand graduates, the School has developed special winter programmes in advanced management courses, as well as in theatre and the arts. The school is now affiliated with the University of Calgary, and since 1972 it has been called 'The Banff Centre'.

In 1937 and 1938, the Federal Government arranged for the designing and construction of the 'Cascades of Time', the beautiful gardens of the Administration grounds; although, as the Opera House was not torn down until the 1940s, the west section was not completed until sometime later. Different rocks used on the different terraces of the gardens were to represent different geological eras. A descriptive tablet was placed on a table in one of the roofed sections, but people defaced it so badly the government removed it, as it could no longer be read. The gardens were another effort of the government to give the visitor pleasure; they are a place of beauty in which to relax and watch the ever-changing light on the mountains. Hundreds of thousands of people do enjoy the gardens every year. A visitor once commented to me, "Imagine all this beauty – and free. Most places you would have to pay." So often the best things *are* free.

As a relief project, a small airfield was put at the base of Cascade in 1934-1936, and it has been used by visiting private planes, as well as local flyers. The air currents in the mountains are tricky and caution has to be used on this landing field.

In 1936, the government built the road to the world famous ski-hill on Mount Norquay. The road provided easy access to the hill to attract the visiting skiers; although, from 1928, the town's people had skied up Stony Squaw Mountain to reach Norquay ski-hill.

The first pair of locally owned skis were sent to George Paris, in 1894, by a guest at the Brett Sanitorium. He was a Norwegian who learned that George liked snowshoeing and thought he should try skiing. George decided the run from the Hot Springs would be just right for a start. On the way down, he had a fall, and one ski was broken. Then and there he concluded he would stick to snowshoes. Conrad Kain, an Austrian guide who came in 1910, had the next pair of skis. He built a very small jump on Tunnel Mountain with very gradual slopes, but most of the skiing was cross-country.

To prepare for the first Winter Carnival, in 1917, some of the local boys made hardwood skis, using part of the round cheese boxes for tips. The harness was a leather strap attached to the ski; broom handles substituted for poles; and any kind of footwear, even moccasins, was used. The only skiing at that Carnival was jumping on the Tunnel Mountain jump on the north side of the mountain, with the runway going toward the Buffalo Paddock. The Scandinavian jumpers came from Camrose, Rossland and Edmonton for the event.

the first ski lodge at Mount Norquay

The following year, Dave White and Company brought in proper skis. The Carnival had both jumping and a cross-country run. Gus Johnson, one of the Camrose jumpers, stayed to teach skiing and help organize the first Ski Club, which was done the same year. The boys cleared slopes on Mount Norquay. When they asked permission from Superintendent Major Jennings to do this, he agreed, but asked them not to cut every tree. Obediently, they left one beautiful pine. Hence 'The Lone Pine' run.

It was not until after World War II that the government undertook to clear the valley. Actually, the first real use of Norquay was by snowshoers, who liked the pass with plenty of snow and sun and well sheltered from the wind.

Owen 'Bugs' Bryant, a Boston entomologist, came to Banff very often in the 1920s. He befriended the young fellows and thought a ski cabin should be built. He arranged with Gus Johnson to cut logs along the edge of the avalanche slope to below the terminus of the present lower chair lift. He piled them where the lower lift building is now, and where the cabin was to be built. That was the summer of 1923 or 1924 – and someone appropriated the logs! Four years later the Ski Club formed a company and built a lodge, on the flat below the present first aid building. That lodge burned down in 1938 and private interests built the present lodge.

The Buffalo ice-carving at the Banff Winter Carnival, executed by Charles Beil.

In 1921, the Banff Winter Carnival joined the pro-ski-jumping circuit which brought many professionals as well as amateurs. In 1929, two British women skiers showed the local skiers how to set up a slalom course. Skins were not used until the 1930s, after a ski party from Boston had used them at Skoki. After 1910, the Canadian Pacific Railway began to advertise Banff as a winter and summer resort and was instrumental in bringing the Dominion Ski Championships to Banff in 1937 and 1940.

In 1930, Skoki Lodge was opened, and before long, it was enlarged by two additions and a small lodge known as the Halfway Hut at the foot of Boulder Pass. This ski area is to be found near Lake Louise. In 1931, Cliff White took a party on the pioneer ski climb on Ptarmigan Glacier to the summit at over ten thousand feet. Vic Kutschera guided Henry S. Kingman of Minneapolis, and later, A.N.T. Rankin of London, England over the same ski area.

Erling Strom, a Norwegian ski-runner, and Marquis Nicholas d'Egli Albizzi were the first outside ski-runners to organize conducted ski tours around Banff. Mount Assiniboine was their favourite area. Nearly a two days' foot journey from Banff, Mount Assiniboine has been a much used area for spring skiing, though now helicopter transport to it has been stopped by regulation.

In 1930, five men skied from Jasper to Banff for the Banff Winter Carnival. Frank Burstrum, Vern Jeffery, A.L. Withers, Doug Jeffery and Joe Weiss had a hard trip; there was heavy snow, and once, on the North Saskatchewan River, they broke through the ice and had to build a fire to clear the skis of ice; the temperature ranged from fifty-five degrees below zero to thirty-five degrees below. No wonder they were four days late! But they arrived at the warden's cabin near the North Saskatchewan bridge just as Wardens U. Lacasse and W. Child were starting out to look for them. From there to Lake Louise the going was good. The trip took two weeks.

In 1932, Russell Bennett of Minneapolis decided to try a ski traverse from the Yellowhead to the Kicking Horse Pass. Bennett was one of the first American ski-runners to look for Alpine-type skiing in the Canadian Rockies. In 1930, he had made an attempt to go from Jasper to Parker Ridge, but exploration on the Columbia Icefields failed because of bad weather and shortage of provisions. For the 1932 trip, he chose Josef Weiss, a Swiss guide in Jasper, and Clifford White of Banff to go with him. Pete Withers went with them as far as Camp Parker Ridge, but he only had a limited time and had to return to Jasper. March was chosen as the best time to avoid blizzards, long periods of sub-zero weather and to have packed, crusted snow. Through the courtesy of officials of Jasper National Park and Banff National Park, and Fred Brewster of Jasper and Jim Simpson of Banff, they were provided with cabins for night stops. They carried a tent for emergencies, and food caches had been made in late September. They left Jasper March 8th and reached Lake Louise March 26th, having gone 300 miles, explored the Athabasca Glacier and climbed the Snow Dome, the apex of the three-way divide from which the waters flow to the Pacific, the Arctic and Hudson Bay.

The Canadian Pacific Railway, like the government, felt the change wrought by the coming of the automobile and, in its advertising, stressed a resort accessible to all. The Company had endless tours, both summer and winter, at special rates. The publicity department, headed by John Murray Gibbon, thought up special events to bring people to Banff (and thus to their other hotels), and played-up these events in worldwide advertising. As early as 1917, J.B. Harkin had tried to have a national travel bureau established, but it was not until 1934 that the Canadian Travel Bureau was created.

In 1924, the Canadian Pacific Railway started the 'Trail Riders of the Canadian Rockies', which was to have a worldwide membership. The government gave encouragement by cutting new trails, such as the Egypt Lake trail to the Banff-Windermere Highway. Every year, a ride was organized, and arrangements made with guides and packers. The ride, for three days, followed trails through mountain passes, past beautiful lakes and along tumbling rivers. The finale was always a big Pow-Wow with campfire and song, much like the one held each night of the ride, when everyone gathered

ice-boating on Lake Minnewanka, 1902

for a song and to listen to tales told by the guides and old timers. Wilf Carter, who had been a packer, started with the Trail Riders at the suggestion of John Murray Gibbon. This was the beginning of Carter's career – singing and playing guitar around the campfires of the Trail Riders in the Canadian Rockies. Today, the Trail Riders use a base camp from which they take short rides each day.

From 1927 to 1930, 'Highland Games' were held on the track next to the tennis courts on the Banff Springs Hotel grounds. Scottish competitors came from all over to compete in hammer throwing, shot put, Highland dancing and bagpipe competitions. For three days, the mountain peaks echoed to the skirl of the pipes. In the evenings, the hotel had entertainment, such as the "Beggars' Opera", or old Scottish and English ballads, for a musical evening. For these, musical artists were brought to Banff. The Canadian Pacific also organized special events, such as the 1929 Championship Track meet. The very costly Banff Springs Golf Course was another one of their successful efforts to attract visitors.

The Canadian Pacific Bungalow Camps at Lake O'Hara, Wapta, Yoho, Emerald Lake, Moraine Lake, Storm Mountain, Vermilion Crossing and Radium Hot Springs, established as a result of car travel, became as well known as the Banff Springs Hotel and Chateau Lake Louise.

What did the residents of Banff do? They built bungalow camps and motels, and increased the number of rooming-houses. Many of these were winterized when skiing and the winter carnival became popular. Homes, gardens and stores were improved; a bowling alley and dance hall were opened. Many more restaurants came into existence – specialty restaurants took the place of the friendly tearoom of earlier days.

The Banff Winter Carnival was one idea that came out of a quiet evening Norman Luxton and Barney W. Collison, Magistrate, spent in the Luxton home in 1917. Together they devised a plan, and the next day, Luxton sent a wire signed by both men to J.B. Harkin who replied that the government would back a Carnival; a similar request to the Canadian Pacific Railway Public Relations office brought the same favourable response. Business men in Banff and several commercial firms in Calgary donated trophies and prizes. The Banff Outdoors Club had built a mile-long toboggan slide, starting on Tunnel Mountain, down Caribou Street to end on the frozen Bow River, in 1916, and that became one regular feature of the Carnivals. The Canadian Pacific Railway ran special trains from Winnipeg, Edmonton and Vancouver to the Banff Carnivals, which became an annual event. There were an Ice Palace and competitions in ski-joring, ski races and jumping, fancy skating and skating races, snow-shoe hikes and races, swimming, toboggan races, dog-sleigh races, whippet races, trap-shooting, as well as hockey matches and a Bonspiel. Ski-joring was popular for both pleasure and in competition. The skier, holding a rope attached to the saddle, followed behind a horse and rider.

Tipi-pitching competition at the Banff Winter Carnival, circa 1927.

The combined intelligence of all three made ski-joring fast and exciting. The technique is similar to water-skiing, with wide swings to the sides.

There were dances every night of the week, with a masquerade on Friday. At midnight on Saturday, the crowning of the next year's queen took place. The Carnival was very colourful and gay, with the town decorated and everyone wearing sport clothes. Good fellowship prevailed among competitors, and visitors and residents all participated in the fun.

In figure skating, two Banff native daughters, Margaret and Mary Simpson, daughters of Jim and Mrs. Billie Simpson, were among the first to attain widespread popularity. The two girls were destined to become known as 'The Sweethearts of the Rockies'. They skated in Madison Square Garden, New York, in Chicago hotels, in night clubs in various cities, and in the Boston Gardens, Boston, where they later became instructors. They performed for Their Majesties King George VI and Queen Elizabeth at the St. Regis Hotel, New York. The girls were sensational as human pin-wheels and noted for beauty of line and grace in their Scottish hunting dances. They planned their own designs and innovations in style. In the summer, Jim, their father, cut and smoothed a rink on Bow Glacier so they could practise. Jim said when he finished he just threw the tools into a crevasse, and then he said, "They will come out at the foot of the glacier some day, rusted, and battered,

Indian Days Parade, 1915, with N.K. Luxton, left

and some visitor will say, 'Goodness! look at the prehistoric ice-scraper I have found!" Jim Simpson built the handsome Num-ti-jah Lodge at Bow Lake, which he and his wife, Billie, managed for years. Jim, with his never-ending supply of stories, and Billie, with her droll sense of humour. delighted many famous guests. Guests came to climb, to paint, to write or to go on packtrips, and some came incognito to enjoy a holiday without being lionized. In 1974, Simpson Mountain on the Banff-Jasper Highway was named in honour of Jim.

In either 1894, or 1897, when there were floods which prevented the trains from running, W.L. Matthews, the manager of the Banff Springs Hotel, asked Tom Wilson for an idea to entertain the stranded guests. This led to the first Banff Indian Days. It seems likely the date would be 1894, when the trains were held for a week, because in 1897 they were held only for three days. After 1902, it became an annual event managed by N.K. Luxton, assisted by J.I. Brewster. Again, the business men and organizations in town, as well as the Canadian Pacific Railway, gave donations. The government donated a buffalo each day for meat, and the grocery merchants of Banff donated other foods such as flour, sugar, tea, bread and jam; other business men gave money. At the end of each afternoon's sports, the chiefs and councillors for each band sat in a circle and members of each band gave out the rations for the band. By the 1930s, the Canadian Pacific Railway and automobiles were bringing thousands of visitors to Indian Days. Of some interest is the fact that all monetary proceeds from the gate went to the Indians in the form of food or prize money for competitions and for the parade; the citizens and organizations of Banff gave voluntary help. Only the Indians rode or walked in the parade, except for the two Mounted Policemen, who rode in the lead, followed by Jim Brewster. It stopped on Banff Avenue extending in length from Wolf Street to across the bridge.

Here the costumes and dog and horse travois were judged, Luxton having ridden ahead to make certain the judges were ready. After the judging, the parade proceeded to the Banff Springs Hotel, where the manager and any visiting dignitaries gave speeches of welcome, while bell boys distributed cigarettes and candy. Afternoons, sports were held at the Indian Camp. In the evenings there were Indian songs, dances and pageants on the Banff Springs grounds. Today, the Kinsmen organize and manage Indian Days.

The Banff Regatta on Victoria Day, the 24th of May, started in the nineties and reached its peak in the 1930s. The races were held on the Bow upstream toward Echo Creek, and the course was decorated with flags and pennants. Day excursions from Edmonton and Calgary were run by the railway for this event. There would frequently be a ball game following the Regatta, and then many visitors would have a swim before starting home. In those early days homes and business places would all have "Union Jacks" flying on the 24th of May and on July 1st.

Lew Cody, cast as a Mountie in The Valley of Silent Men, 1922, on location at the site of the present Tunnel Mountain Campground.

In 1888, curling started in Banff with one sheet of ice in front of the Brett Sanitorium Hotel. They had two rinks going by 1899, with John Walker, Dave White, Frank Beattie, Dr. Brett, Bill Mather, Ike Byers, Mr. Galletly and Dr. White (Brett's assistant). Later, Bill Mather, who ran the boat house and open air skating rink, decided to flood the draw between the recreation grounds and the Bow River. This gave room for six or eight sheets and the Banff Curling Club was formed. Bonspiels started and brought visitors. A temporary rink with a high wire fence was located on Marten Street until 1920, when a large enclosed curling club was finished on Birch Avenue. Finally, in the early 1960s the present one was built in the community centre across the tracks.

The motion picture industry has long found Banff, Lake Louise, Moraine Lake and Jasper ideal locations for their productions. Local people and the Swiss guides helped many times as stand-ins or in crowd scenes. In 1922, a movie made by Cosmo Productions, starring Alma Rubens, was filmed on Mount Norquay and at Lake Minnewanka. In 1923 a Strongheart movie, "The Silent Partner", was made, with Harold Austin and Mary Astor, at Lake Minnewanka and Banff. The company donated the Strongheart Trophy to the dog-team races held on Lake Minnewanka that year instead of at The Pas, Manitoba. "The Alaskan" with Walter Brennan, Estelle Taylor (the first Mrs. Jack Dempsey) and Anna May Wong was filmed at Castle while Joe Smith was living there. He took part in some scenes. About the same time, Edward Feuz, the Swiss guide, helped in a Lew Cody, and Alma Rubens movie on the Tunnel Mountain rifle range. In 1936-1937, British Gaumont film company made "The Great Barrier" based on Allan Sullivan's novel The Great Divide, the story of the building of the Canadian Pacific Railway, starring Richard Arlen and Lilli Palmer.

"The King of the Mountains", one of John Barrymore's movies, directed by Ernest Lubitsch, was made in 1928 in Banff and on Victoria Glacier at Lake Louise. Camilla Horne, the daughter of a Banff resident, starred opposite Barrymore, and Rudolf Aemmer, one of the Swiss guides, doubled for Barrymore in glacier shots. Jim Boyce, a local guide and outfitter for thirty years, who had a dog-team of his own, took part in the "Winds of Chance", filmed on the Plain of Six Glaciers, and in "The Silent Partner" and "The Branding Iron". When "The Trail of '98" by Robert Service was being filmed out of Denver and San Pedro, Jim took seventy-five sleigh dogs to the United States to take part in it. In 1954-1955, wardens Christensen, Hermanrude, Tasker, Woodworth and Green were involved in an animal picture produced by the Walt Disney Studios of Hollywood. These are a few of the movies made here, which, in their fashion, carried scenes of Banff and the parks to many places in the world.

XV

Sidelights

I have taken you through the environmental changes and the growth of Banff, but nowhere have I presented its physical image. The frontier town of the 1880s and 1890s had small log buildings and shacks with roofs of hand-hewn shingles made from the natural materials at hand. The hotels had wide verandahs with plenty of chairs, so visitors or locals could look at Banff Avenue, survey the mountains or chat. Frame houses of one or two stories came next; the lumber for these came from Calgary mills. These houses were not distinctive in architecture except for steep roofs to shed the snow. Sometimes the roofs were adorned with the kind of scroll work that we call "gingerbread" trim, which was fashionable at the time. Bungalows and semi-bungalows with fireplaces were popular for permanent residences, or for summer homes at a later date, and some of these were of log construction. Cobblestone (fieldstone) was used very little except for trim and verandah pillars. In a later period, stucco with Rundle Stone trim became popular for both houses and business blocks. Brick, owing to its high cost, was not used extensively. The short-lived period of tent-houses and cabin-shacks was a temporary setback when building could not keep up with the number of visitors, and money was scarce in the 1930s.

Like Topsy, Banff 'just growed'. Building regulations were introduced from time to time. Many of them were unquestionably good, but they were not always followed, and the attempts to make Banff into an Alpine-type town failed. No one really was to blame. Good intentions always cost money, and lack of funds has always been a problem in Banff, both to residents and government. More than once the government brought in expensive, clever town planners, but unforeseen contingencies made it impossible to bring their projects to fruition. At least, rigid regulations in opening lots for occupation have kept Banff compact and eliminated the worst of haphazard development. Over the years, a community pride has developed, and both people and government have endeavoured to fit the town into its surroundings. Today, unfortunately, modern architectural trends are more and more obvious in

Banff, and however suitable these may be in large urban centres, they produce disharmony rather than harmony in a mountain environment.

Before the World Wars, Banff residents were mainly English and Scottish, many of whom came from Eastern Canada as well as the British Isles. From the beginning, there have been Chinese, who worked in mines, provided restaurants and had stores. Most of them were fine men who made their contribution to town progress and development by committee work, subscriptions and by bringing their beautiful crafts to Banff. There was once a young Japanese man who had a large shop on Banff Avenue that sold the products of craftsmen of Japan. Then there was James (Bill) Davie, whose parents had once been slaves. He came to Canada in 1904, and finally reached Banff in 1911 and remained here. Bill did many jobs, then he married Jessie E. Ellis of London, England, in 1914. Bill finally had his own confectionary and shoeshine shop on Banff Avenue. He was the only Negro who ever lived in Banff, and was one of the well-liked and respected citizens. After the First World War, a small number of Europeans made their homes in Banff, and after the Second World War, the population was swelled by many more. Today, many nationalities are represented in business and in various activities in Banff.

Banff has always had an atmosphere of cosmopolitanism because the early visitors came from all over the world. In those days and into the 1920s, summer visitors came from Europe, the British Isles, the United States and the Orient; winter travellers were more often Australians. These people imparted an air of worldliness to Banff and its residents, and broadened their outlook. The people living with this vicarious cosmopolitanism thought big and planned big.

Today with cars, bus lines and airplanes, the visitors still come from all over the world, winter and summer. They enjoy all the early travellers did, but with many more facilities; however, they miss the intimacy, or the feeling of belonging, that the early visitors were given. Sad to say, today's visitor always seems aware of time and is in a hurry. Among the Banff people a sense of commercialism has developed and destroyed the delightful hospitality and fellowship that Banff once gave. No one person is responsible; it is just one of the changes which inevitably follows in the wake of progress.

The following people, incidents, happenings and efforts of some people and organizations have been chosen not because they are particularly outstanding, but because they show a little of the development of Banff through the years. There are many parallels to these in other families, other efforts and other events in Banff's history, but all cannot be cited. The town residents, although of necessity tourist-conscious, have had their private lives. Banff, like every town, has had its eccentrics, its money-grubbers, its idealists and its generous folk. It has had its poor, and its n'er-do-wells, its unfortunates and those who have prospered. Generally speaking, it has not

Sir Charles G.D. Roberts with Walking Buffalo at the Banff Indian Days

had its 'town drunk', but it has had hard drinkers. Most interesting among the comments of early visitors were the very many which underlined the fact that George E. Stewart, the park's first superintendent, kept remarkably good order. Visitors observed that although there were bars, these being in almost every Banff hotel, no one ever came across completely inebriated persons. Not that the people of Banff have been saintly; they have had their petty grievances, jealousies and animosities, but generally, on larger issues, they have always presented a united front.

In many ways Banff followed the social patterns and practises of any small town. For years, on summer Sunday evenings, people walked to the railway station to see the train come in with its visitors. This was a social occasion when news and gossip were exchanged. After the train pulled out, some people wandered home, while others went to the ice cream parlour. The 'silk trains' used to roar through on their non-stop trips, heralding their approach with a long blast of the whistle at the west crossing and fading into the distance at the east crossing. These trains, now things of the past, had top priority on any railroad. Speed was essential to get the raw silk from China to the manufacturer before it would spoil. The silk trains generally came through Banff during the night, but because the engineers had all stops wide open, were unmistakable.

There was a time when many tramps used to ride the trains. They, too, would stop off in Banff. The 'station bush' was their favourite hang-out. Those men would come to the houses and ask for food but they never caused any trouble. The greatest danger from them was that they might accidentally set the bush on fire. After a short stay they would move on, riding the rods on another train. The 'station bush' has long since been replaced by houses.

Before the days of automobiles, runaways were exciting, and it was not unusual to see a carriage careering down Main Street behind a lathered team. Men sitting on the hotel verandahs or standing on the street would dash out to grab the head straps, if possible. Visitors enjoyed this kind of excitement, but sometimes other things happened to them, too. One July day in 1903, four ladies were driving along the Loop Road when one looked back and saw a mountain lion trailing them, about a hundred yards behind. One lady exclaimed it was fourteen feet long, another said it was the size of an elephant and the visitor next to the driver said it was the size of an ordinary buffalo! The driver, showing great presence of mind, stated that atmospheric conditions caused unacclimatized, people to be deceived in regard to size and distance and that the animal was only of the ordinary size. When the ladies reached the Banff Springs Hotel and told their story, many of the guests called for saddle-horses. Of course, when the riders, after a wild dash, arrived at the spot, they only saw the tracks where the animal had turned into the bush. Such were the events that made a visitor's day exciting.

In the early days Banff had its dairies; not until comparatively recently, did the big companies take over. John Brewster, who came to Banff in 1887 from Kingston, Ontario, had started a dairy at the corner of Banff Avenue and Moose Street. In 1896 he moved it across the tracks north of the present railway station. He later sold it to Frank Wellman, who in turn sold it in 1911 to C.W. Moffat, who came to Banff in 1910. Moffat had the dairy for twenty-seven years, then sold it to the Union Milk Company in 1938. A fire destroyed the barn that John Brewster had moved from his first location shortly before the sale. Moffat kept his lease and continued to live in his home at the old dairy site. John Brewster's family have been associated with the parks ever since, although John himself and his sons left at various times to try other fields. Probably Jim stayed the most with the Banff business, and it was he who built the first ski lodge at Sunshine. The Moffat family, too, have stayed and participated in Banff's growth. Others who had dairies came and went. Of the largest companies, Union Milk was here until it recently was absorbed into another concern.

Cory Duncan had an early dairy at Anthracite, then he moved the dairy to Duthill, but continued his Banff deliveries. One winter night, he was going home along the King's Highway when a lynx dropped down on him from an overhanging tree. The horses took fright, and Gory and the lynx had a struggle, but finally, Cory got his head and shoulders under the animal and heaved him out of the sleigh. Cory did not get the frightened horses under control until he reached the bottom of Anthracite Hill, which was nearly home. When asked how he felt about the incident, Cory said, "Well, I guess I didn't like the smell any better than the team did."

An English lady who came to Banff in the very early 1900s was Miss Bertha E. Kyte Reynolds. She stayed and wrote for English magazines and played the organ in the Anglican Church for many years. Her home, above the Bow River, was a tent in the woods beyond the old cemetery. She used to gather her firewood on Tunnel Mountain. This short, energetic, and 'very English' woman used to take long walks. It was a usual sight to see her, clad in an English tweed suit, wearing stout walking shoes, striding along with her walking stick in all seasons. Finally, the government forbade her to live in her tent, because tents were forbidden in town, and told her she must go outside the park to Canmore. Instead, Miss Reynolds moved to Victoria and lived in a cabin of Mrs. George Fowles, near Cadboro Bay. The George Fowles' were old friends, who had retired from Banff some time before.

Kyte Reynolds, as she was known, was a remittance woman. Her family gave her a little money to live in Banff; fortunately, the people were good to her, and she managed to exist. One of the Anglican clergymen, on sabbatical in England, visited her home. He told her relations they must increase her allowance; that she would starve except for the Banff people. Her pension came in later years and helped a little. When she was ninety-five years old, a brother in South Africa, who had lost track of her, left her a very large legacy. Through newspapers and other inquiries, his executors found her, but like so many things it came too late, for she died three years after at ninety-seven. Not until then did people learn she was related to the Most Reverend William Temple, Archbishop of Canterbury.

Another English woman who became well known was Miss Ethel Unwin, who arrived from the Old Country in 1907 to visit her brother Sidney, who was already well known as a packer. She has given some of her impressions of Banff as she first saw it. "It was a Banff Indian Day and the Indians were riding along Main Street in full dress. The street had wooden sidewalks and spruce trees were planted down the middle. There were only a few buildings. A narrow road led to the Buffalo Park next to which the sports were held; and west of Banff there was only a pony trail to Laggan. In a few days I went by train to Glacier to manage a gift shop for Sid Baker, a friend of my brother. The trains stopped there for meals. I left for England in December."

In 1909, she returned and rented a house on Beaver Street next to the Anglican Church, where she ran a boarding house. She had a happy time; in the summer she and her friends rowed, canoed, and played tennis, and in the winter they skated and snow-shoed. There were jolly moonlight parties, when the boys would go during the day and arrange the place for the night picnic and the sing-song.

In 1912, she, and her brother, Sid, had a gift shop next to the Paris Tea-room but the war came in 1914; the bottom fell out of the business and her brother was killed overseas so she sold it.

The next year, she moved to a house which her brother had built near the cemetery and looked after the four flats it contained. In 1917, she caused a real commotion in the town. She took two of the girls staying in one of the flats to climb Rundle Mountain, and they all got trapped. The alarm was turned in the next day, and many of the people turned out to search for the missing women. Finally, in the afternoon, they were found, and by evening were back home. Miss Unwin was the first woman in Banff to have a guide's license, and, in 1918, she took a party on a short trip. She decided guiding was not for her, so she disposed of the horses and gave it up. Miss Unwin sold her home and travelled in England and Europe for some time, only to return to Banff in 1922, when she started an Odd Craft Shop and ran it until 1947. She finally returned to England.

Although Mr. and Mrs. Henry Greenham were not real old-timers, they contributed very much to the community work. Miss Margaret Haskins came from England to Canada in 1914 to be Headmistress at Havergal Ladies College in Toronto. There she taught English and Dramatics. Mr. Greenham, an Oxford graduate, came to Canada in 1910 to the Pine Lake District in Alberta. There he had a small trading post and taught in the country school.

In 1919, Miss Haskins came to the Alpine Club in Banff; she was standing at a scenic point overlooking Bow Valley and murmured, 'How beautiful'. Mr. Henry Greenham was standing beside her and it was love at first sight, not only of each other, but also of Banff. They were married and came back in 1920 to start the Mountain School. Such a school in mountain surroundings had been their individual dreams, and together they made it come true.

Mrs. Greenham, Mrs. Jim Simpson and Mrs. Ernest Kennedy organized the Banff Literary Dramatic Club in 1923. Mrs. Greenham urged the club members, after it was formed, to think of it as a study group. Membership was a dollar a year, and the club grew rapidly. The men and women met at different homes one evening a week, to read and to discuss plays. Mrs. Greenham started with the Little Theatre Movement and they discussed such plays as: 'Land of Heart's Desire' by William Butler Yeats, 'Riders to the Sea' by J.M. Synge and 'Work House Ward' by Lady Gregory. Later they produced plays, not only during the group meetings, but in the Bretton Hall Theatre and went on to compete in the annual Drama Festival.

Mrs. Margaret Greenham's Children's Theatre

Mrs. Greenham organized the 'Merry-Go-Round' Theatre for children at the School of Fine Arts, which she carried on until 1959. The 'Margaret Greenham Theatre' at the School of Fine Arts was named in memory of her.

Mr. and Mrs. Greenham took pleasure in community efforts and helped during the Carnival and Indian Days. Both were ardent mountain climbers, and they used their holidays for camping halfway down Lake Minnewanka, on the north shore in a beautiful aspen park. Mr. Greenham's poem 'The Great Adventure' reflects the influence of the mountains on his life and thought. They both loved the wild birds, animals and flowers.

Once, when a current wedding was being discussed after a dramatic club meeting, Mr. Greenham said to her, "Do you remember your wedding bouquet? I went into the woods and picked all the wild flowers I could find." She smiled and replied, "It was the loveliest bouquet I ever saw."

In Banff, the Royal Canadian Legion played a very significant role in town affairs. Looking back over their many activities, one realizes how typical these were of Banff as a whole. It was the period of picnics, sleigh-rides, dances and sports. The Whist Drives were replacing the old box-socials from earlier days, when each lady would spend much time and thought on cooking as well as decorating her box for her partner at the dance. These boxes were raffled and the highest bidder became the lady's partner; doubtless, the young men often had a whispered hint from their particular friends before the bidding started. By tracing the history of the legion, one realizes the parallel development of other town organizations such as Rotary, Kinsmen, Shriners and Kiwanis.

In 1968, the Rocky Mountains Park Branch of the Royal Canadian Legion celebrated its fiftieth anniversary. Founded in 1917, the first eighteen members soon became thirty; William Noble was President and some of the members came from Canmore.

At first, they held their meetings in the old Banff Fire Hall, then they moved into a room over Dave White's store. After decorating that club room, they opened with a Whist Drive and dance. Soon after, they had Whist Drives, dances, bazaars, auction sales, raffles and baby shows to raise funds to build a Memorial Hall. Once they had a Basket Picnic at Healy Creek; sometimes the Overseas Club joined in their efforts. Donations from members and the town tradesmen enabled them to buy a lot on Banff Avenue. The Memorial Hall opened in 1923, but only the basement because the upstairs was not completed until later.

From the beginning, Armistice Day was observed with parades and services, and the cenotaphs, at Bankhead, built in 1921, and at Banff, built in 1923, were decorated; there were also Armistice banquets and concerts.

In 1924, the giant Christmas Tree for all the children under fourteen in the community was started. By 1926, the Legion found they could not continue to sponsor the community tree, so they had one for members' children only, until 1945, when other organizations joined to have a community tree. Finally, only the Legion and Kinsmen were left and they had the community tree until 1961. Since then the Legion has had a pre-school children's community tree.

During the 'hungry thirties' many men, including veterans, worked on building the Mount Norquay Road, one of the government relief projects. Some of the veterans went to relief camps called 'National Defence Camps'; one was on the east road in the park, others at Canmore, Morley, the Gap and Cochrane. Unlike the situation in most Canadian towns in the depression years, Banff business went on pretty much as usual. The volume of business was less, but there were no bankruptcies. There were few references in the newspapers to the depression, but it was noted that there was a decrease in traffic in 1929. In January 1931, it was reported, "Perhaps it is not as bright as in past years, but it is far from a black outlook." With a feeble effort at psychology, the press urged people to "think and act prosperity". Later that year, the depression was deepening with the result that few Canadians were travelling. In December, 1931, work on the Banff-Jasper road came to a halt because of lack of funds. Then on January 1, 1932, the order was reversed to provide employment. Although everyone economized during these years, the overall hardship was not extreme. The results of two very wet summers or times when fires were bad in the 1920s had been just as devastating to business as the depression.

In May, 1935, the Legion and other clubs in Banff commemorated the Silver Jubilee of Their Majesties King George V and Queen Mary, with a large parade. Banff Boer War veterans and veterans of the Great War marched in that parade. In 1936, the Legion took part in the parade for the visit of Governor-General Lord Tweedsmuir and Lady Tweedsmuir. The following year, the Legion took part in the parade to celebrate the Coronation of Their Majesties King George VI and Queen Elizabeth. In the Legion section, veterans of the Great War and the Boer War were joined by Major Bagley and Norman Sanson, who were veterans of the North West Rebellion. The Legion float took first prize in the parade.

In the First World War, enlistments were so heavy the Federal Government and business people had trouble getting men for the necessary work. An interesting story of the Armistice was told by Charlie McAuley. When the 1918 Armistice was to be signed, Kina Sibbald, the telephone operator, kept in touch with Calgary to get the news as soon as possible. Meanwhile, Dave White had arranged for a number of young fellows to bring a lot of the defunct privies from all over Banff and pile them at the King Edward Hotel corner. Charlie McAuley and Dan McCowan put two high school children on to ring each church bell. As soon as the news came the bells rang, and the bonfire burned all night; and there was another bonfire built by some others on top of Tunnel Mountain. As Charlie McAuley said, Banff really got tidied up that night, and practically everyone in town was at the King Edward corner. During the Second World War, 1939 to 1945, Banff had a record for enlistments per capita. There were 411 enlistments altogether in all the Services, of which forty-five were women. In May 1947, the Ladies Auxiliary was formed. The original Memorial Hall burned in January 1961, and the fire gutted a new addition built two years earlier. By January, 1962, the building, as it is today, was finished.

Through the years, the Legion carried on community projects and sponsored many causes. In 1967, Centennial Year, they put up the money to make a project possible. This money purchased equipment for a new children's playground in the Recreation Grounds. Plans by Banff citizens for other town projects had been thwarted by government rulings.

On the fiftieth anniversary of the Legion, a birthday dinner was held, and Mrs. Pearl Moore unveiled a plaque which officially changed the name to 'Colonel Moore Branch' of the Royal Canadian Legion to honour Philip Moore, a charter member and one of the old-timers of Banff.

The Banff Public Library was started in 1949 by the Junior Chamber of Commerce and the Jaycettes, and was under the direction of Mrs. Marjorie Jamieson. Books were contributed by residents of Banff, and the library was in the basement of the Banff Clinic. As it grew, the library moved to a house on Bear Street. Then Mrs. Peter (Catharine) Whyte and the directors of the Peter Whyte Foundation decided to build there and the house containing the library was moved to the parking lot across the street. The new building, designed by Philip Delesalle of Calgary, a very handsome and functional one, was to house not only the library but an archives and an art gallery. Mrs. Whyte already had an archivist, Mrs. Maryalice Stewart, a native of Banff and related to the Brewster family, who had been collecting archival material for the proposed 'Archives of the Canadian Rockies'.

Finally, in June, 1968, the beautiful building was opened as Mrs. Whyte's gift to Banff. Dr. Charles Beil was the speaker for the occasion. He said it was a very great addition to Banff and the records would become invaluable. He went on to say if one relaxed in the building he might hear "the echo of a pack-train clacking against the stones, as it wound its way up a rocky trail or the early morning tinkle of a bell-mare." He continued, saying many of the good old story-tellers were silent now, but they would live on in records kept in the archives, and be preserved forever. He then introduced Jim Simpson, one of the early pioneers and outfitters of Banff. Mr. Simpson spoke of Mrs. Whyte's generosity and advised the young people to use the contents of the building well. "You are all born with an equal chance of improving yourselves, but don't be fooled by greatness. Here is a cheque from one of the important financial institutions of our country, signed with important names, but it isn't worth a damn without my name on it. So you see, a lot who appear great are

the Archives of the Canadian Rockies

not as great as they think they are." Then Jim took his hunting knife and cut the buckskin ribbon, and declared the Archives of the Canadian Rockies officially opened.

The crowd of several hundred people, including Stony Indians from Morley, toured the building where an exhibition of Peter Whyte's paintings was on display in the art gallery. Now people come from all over the world to do research, see exhibitions or enjoy a cup of tea in front of the fireplace. Bill Peyto's and Bill Mather's and Jack Sinclair's log cabins have been moved to the grounds of the Peter Whyte Foundation, as it is called today; more recently, the log home of Colonel Philip Moore has also been moved there. This was done so that these buildings would be preserved for the future.

Norman Luxton, all his life, had a dream of showing the life, customs and crafts of the Plains Indians to white people so that they would have a better understanding of the Indian and his culture. Luxton worked with Indians as a young boy in Manitoba and continued to do so when he came to Banff in 1902. Over the years, he collected Indian artifacts, but not until 1951 did he build the first log building to start the now famous Luxton Museum. The next year, he moved the old Banff Gun Club building, which he had built himself, to adjoin the museum as a caretaker's residence. In 1952, the workshop was added, followed by a second exhibit room. Then, Mr. Eric Harvie, a Calgary lawyer and philanthropist, became interested, much as he was to become interested at a later date in the School of Fine Arts. By 1958, the fort, the largest room of all, had come into being. Life-size mannequins of Indians, with faces modelled from live subjects, are used to show types of dress and depict how the Indians worked, played, danced and travelled. Artists, designers, researchers and visitors come by the thousands to see the museum. When Mr. Luxton died, he left the Luxton Museum to the Glenbow Foundation founded by Mr. Harvie. The Luxton Museum now belongs to the Alberta Provincial Government.

The old-timers were pioneers who knew what hardship and hard work meant. They were interesting people with a well-developed sense of humour, which they sorely needed. There was a feeling of good fellowship and kindness in community interests and toward visitors. Being practically isolated, these people developed self-sufficiency and met fun or disaster with equanimity. They were not perfect, but Banff people today can look back on that generation with some pride. Through this history, I have mentioned a number of people only as they were connected with the development of Banff; many others worked along similar lines, but to do all the pioneer Banff families justice another book would have to be written.

Today, everything has changed in Banff. Travellers no longer have to be induced to come by arranging special events such as the Highland Games or the Winter Carnival. They come by the thousands in trailers, campers, automobiles and buses. Now the government, the Canadian Pacific hotel and the residents have to supply the facilities to meet these new demands. More campgrounds, motels, hotels, service stations, grocery stores, restaurants and coin laundries are required. Good roads, swimming pools, launches and canoes are pressing demands. Today's travellers, like those at the turn of the century, want to explore by foot, ski or automobile.

The government has need of more money for upkeep of roads, camps and public utilities. The Canadian Pacific no longer stands for power; it competes for travellers as every other company does. The residents are concerned with supplying the travellers with accommodation, food and incidental amusements or needs, but something of the old spirit has disappeared.

The government and the residents are aware of the need for expansion. But how and where? Land in Banff is very limited. It is probable that more buildings could be constructed higher on the mountain slopes, but this would destroy much of the natural setting of Banff. Where the water used to flow, from the Middle Springs on the flat east of the Hot Springs road near the middle Spring turnoff, among trees and bushes, was a beauty spot. There, orchids such as the lady's slipper, Calypso and round-leaved orchid, as well as mountain lilies and liverwort, used to grow. Now they are gone. Is that the kind of development needed? Will the answer lie in peripheral expansion

Banff Avenue in the early days

just outside park boundaries, or will the far valleys be opened to exploitation? Will the end of natural fuels be nature's response to the automobile age, or will there be some other way nature will protect its own for future generations of the Canadian people? How to preserve the Parks for the enjoyment of all the Canadian people and for future generations, yet at the same time offer the amenities is the question before the government and Park residents today.

XVI

The Future

Control in Banff National Park has been firmly held by the Federal Government from the beginning. Through land lease, building regulations and business licenses it has controlled land use. Its advertising on the other hand has helped make Banff an international resort. The federal authorities supply the municipal services: garbage collection, water and sewer lines, upkeep and construction of roads and sidewalks, cemeteries, traffic regulations and signs, surface drainage, sanitation and public conveniences.

Banff residents pay garbage, water and sewer taxes, and land rent to defray a very small part of the total expenses. They buy business licenses or permits. From the beginning, they have been free to manage their own businesses, once established. The chief difficulty has been, and up to the present still is, that the resident has no voice in formulating government rulings. Policy-making is centralized in Ottawa, and it is frustrating to wait for long-delayed decisions. There is the Western Branch of the Parks Department in Calgary, but it does not have the power to make final decisions without reference to Ottawa. Land rents are an unhappy example – much could be said on both sides, and has been. Possibly, if Ottawa had made reasonable adjustments to the rents, there might have been no problem. The Banff Citizens' Council was formed on February 28, 1921, by permission of Senator James Lougheed, to act in an advisory capacity in affairs in the National Parks. The Banff Advisory Council which grew out of the Citizens' Council on April 7, 1925 acts as an intermediary, between the government and the people, but has no power other than real persistence and suggestion, power which, at times, has had influence.

The Canadian Pacific Railway still co-operates with the government and the people, but its monopoly position is long past. Today its advertising is as valuable to the parks and Banff as it used to be. The Railway Company has competition from the automobile, but uses it, by opening its hotel doors to conventions and tours, winter or summer, and by having special evening entertainment to attract the casual visitor on weekends.

Rocky Mountain Goats, at the Buffalo Park near Banff, 1926

The Federal Government is faced with a problem today that is vital to Banff and to all the parks. This difficulty started when the first visitor was encouraged to come to Rocky Mountains Park. Today more municipal services and facilities are needed for visitors. They must have winter and summer recreation, and places to ski or run the snowmobiles; or have quiet spots to relax in comfortable surroundings, where they may meditate on the wonders and mysteries of nature. Should the Federal Government open more trails and roads into the wilderness? Allow more accommodation to be built?

Parks are reserves where the beauty of scenery and wild life must be preserved, insofar as man is capable of doing it. Nothing is static in nature, but the government has a duty to prevent as much change as possible, while still making the parks available to the people. Should the Federal Government preserve the so-called wilderness for scientific research and nature lovers?

Only the future can answer these vital questions. By judicious land control, no doubt, the Federal Government will manage conservation and plan for the visitor, as well as the residents, in the National Parks of Canada.

Epilogue

In this beautiful valley where the towering peaks, with their glaciers, feel the gentle Chinook or the frigid wind of winter, the lakes reflect the fiery glory of sunrise or the amethyst of sunset. Here the Cascade, tossing rainbows into the air, drops thousands of feet, to disappear mysteriously to seek the subterranean channel to the river. The black bear and the coyote still prowl at night, but in the day, the deer and the Bighorn walk majestically. 'Nature, History, Romance and Indian Legend linger here.'

Despite the continuous tearing and breaking by the elements, and the flash of lightning and the forest fire, this valley will be here for generations to come. We have modified it for our use, but we, the people of Canada and our Federal Government must become aware – and must learn to value beauty. Only cataclysmic change wrought by man or nature could end it all. Only then would the story be ended and all would be gone – gone.

Appendix

The Pablo Buffalo Herd

[The following is an unpublished manuscript written by Norman K. Luxton in 1912.]

One day, Howard Douglas blew into my office and asked me if I wanted to buy a thousand head of buffalo. For a second I thought he was having a joke in his usual dry way, then I saw he meant every word as he gave me a letter to read. A man in Montana, Alexander Ayotte, Canadian Immigration Agent at Missoula, told Douglas there were a thousand head of buffalo on the Flathead Reservation in Montana. He said the owner Michel Pablo wanted to sell them. He had been running them along his cattle range for some years.

It seems the foundation of the Flathead herd dated back to 1873 or 1874 when Walking Coyote, a Pend d'Oreille Indian, known as Samuel, captured four buffalo calves; two heifers and two bulls. Coyote and his family had been hunting where Buffalo, Montana is today. These four calves pathetically followed the hunters when their mothers were killed. They went with Coyote to the St. Ignacious Mission and became pets. By 1884, they had bred to thirteen head. Coyote found them expensive and decided to sell. Mr. D. McDonald, Hudson's Bay Factor on the Flathead Reservation, negotiated with Coyote. Meantime, C.A. Allard who ranched nearby, became impressed with the possibility of a profitable investment. Allard was a shrewd, far-seeing business man. He interested his friend, a fellow rancher Michel Pablo in the project. They bought ten of Walking Coyote's buffalo, and paid 250 dollars per head.

In 1893, Allard and Pablo bought twenty-six pure-bred buffalo and eighteen cattalos from Buffalo Jones, Omaha. This brought their herd to thirty-six thoroughbreds. Buffalo Jones had bought his from Col. Bedson of Stoney mountain, who had bought them from the Hon. James McKay, at one time a provincial secretary of Manitoba. Part of this herd from the Manitoba

145

prairies was bought by Lord Strathcona for Silver Heights, his Winnipeg estate.

Ayotte's letter interested me tremendously, and for a long time Howard and I talked over how to approach the Minister of the Interior, the Hon. Frank Oliver. It was not until I made a trip to Winnipeg and had a two-day session with him, that he consented to start negotiations with the Pablo interests.[1] These interests turned out to be a very large bank in Missoula. An agreement was made wherein Pablo was to deliver his buffalo to Elk Island Park, Alberta. Pablo was to receive ninety dollars per head, unloaded and in good physical condition.

Howard Douglas, Superintendent, Alex Ayotte, a Free Press writer, and I left Calgary for Montana. The only thing I remember of interest on the trip was getting off at the stations to examine the bullet holes in the platform, put there by cowboys making tenderfeet dance. We arrived at Missoula and drove to the Mission. We met Pablo there and drove to Buffalo Camp twenty miles out. This consisted of one log building, the home for the buffalo herder, his wife and family; a sod stable and some corrals.

The cowboys had started to arrive and when we got there some thirty-five cowboys with their saddle-horses and remounts were gathered around. All these fellows were of mixed blood. I often counted more than eighty riders when later on we were organized with young Charles Allard's bunch. I never have seen a finer group of riders or a better herd of horses.

We had brought our own tents and camp supplies. Pablo's chuckwagon served out the meals. After a few days we found it more convenient to live at the Mission and eat home-cooked meals.

Shortly after dinner the first day, the cowboys decided to find out what the Canadians were like. I had brought my own saddle and one of the boys asked me if I cared to pick out a horse or two. I accepted his "kind" thought and in no time, they had a long legged, dark grey saddled. He stood quietly while I got on, but I hardly had my feet in the stirrups when he let go, off the ground in a leap that would have puzzled a jack-rabbit. Only my well-built saddle kept me from going off over his tail. Then it was not so bad. I never was a bronc buster. Why I was not pitched off more than once that day was more good luck than good riding; however that lucky ride did me more good in the estimation of those cowboys than if I had presented them with a keg of liquor.

Mr. Douglas had told me to inspect the house for a possible bed. While the house was clean, as one could wish for, I told the lady I thought we would probably sleep in our own tent, which I reported to Mr. Douglas. Alex Ayotte had a different opinion and gladly paid a week in advance for the room. Now

---

[1] Luxton makes no mention here that his arguments for bringing the buffalo back were conservation, tourist attraction and a possible source of food for the Indians.

Ayotte had been in our company for almost a month, first in Banff and then in Calgary. He weighed 275 pounds, every ounce a tissue of selfishness added to an over-bearing manner. That night Douglas retired early, Ayotte and I sat at the fire listening to the cowboys telling stories and singing. When I saw Ayotte leave for the house I hiked for the tent. I always carried a small twenty-bore shotgun on my trips to collect natural history specimens. Taking two shells I cut them in half leaving only the thin cardboard wad holding the powder. I accidentally wakened Howard, so I started to tell him what I thought would happen, when we heard Ayotte come from the direction of the house, talking and swearing in French. I gave Howard a night lantern to open toward the door. In a second or two it happened. Ayotte all but tore the tent-flap off, we saw his face splashed with dead bed-bugs, and I pulled one trigger. I fired the second shot as Ayotte was scrambling to his feet and running as he probably hadn't done for some years. If Ayotte had gotten into the tent and tumbled on Howard and me it would have been too bad for both of us. Alex slept in the stable from then on. Our night's show amused the cowboys and raised us in their estimation. They laid themselves out to help us in any way they could.

Preparing for the round-up, the buffalo were marked as to number and area of the country they covered grazing. Then Pablo took charge, heading out with thirty-five or forty cowboys. Then he directed each to his position. This took the shape of a horseshoe, with the buffalo between the ends. No noise, no smoking and careful riding allowed the riders to come closer to the buffalo, until they were bunched. Then the slow trek forward. Sometimes these rides went without trouble. Just about the time we thought we would really get them off their regular ground, suddenly, the whole herd would halt as if by command. They would turn around and face the way we had come, stand, not an animal moving in perhaps the hundred we had been following. All the cowboy's horses stood – no sound. Then from a jump start the buffalo would charge right into the horse-shoe of riders, never swerving, as if possessed with the devil riding them. Never once was this charge broken, nothing stopped them, not even the river. It took days to throw them back across the river in dribs and drabs, perhaps a dozen at a time to start again.

As we worked we learned. We found if we had more cows and fewer bulls we would get them to Ravalli. A bunch of cows was a sure bet except when we picked up a real renegade and what she did – phew! Finally, we got them started for Ravalli.

Loading these animals, cows a thousand or more pounds, and bulls over two thousand was a real job. Patience was the password. The corrals were so constructed that the big herd was in the main corral. From this the animals were cut out into a small corral with a chute leading from it into the box car.

These cars were specially built and reinforced from every angle, with an iron water trough running down one side, holding several barrels of water. A strong gate, six feet high and the width of the car, was tied on one side only by a heavy rope, at intervening spaces at four feet apart. The tie was where the buffalo's head would be when in place. These gates were flat against the car so the other end could swing into place at the buffalo's tail-end and were tied from outside the car. The joke was to get the buffalo into the car, for that matter it was a joke to get a buffalo to any wanted place. From the small corral an animal was pushed and prodded up the chute, a little more than half way up his head went into a lariat loop. The other end of the rope was trailed through the car to the position where the buffalo would stand, then outside where the rope was snubbed around a heavy post. Here two or three men operated the slack as a buffalo came in and was in place, then the rope was tied on the outside of the car to stay until it reached Canada. Feeding was done twice a day and watering so the troughs were never empty. With the buffalo in place, the gate, that was already tied at the buffalo's head, was pushed across the car and tied at the buffalo's stern from the outside.

One bull went straight through the car, he just took the side out as if it had not been there. Another bull broke his legs – well, the Indians had a feast out of that.

Another bull nearly did for poor Ayotte, Douglas and McMullen, a C.P.R. man. They were watching a bull go up the chute and the rope broke. Luckily for the fellows the bull's legs slipped and they got over the fence. McMullen got a broken arm when he fell. After he came to, Ayotte went back of the car I was standing on and suddenly that car shook as if by earthquake. One of the onlookers fell on Ayotte's head. We didn't see him anymore that day.

The drive to Ravalli was about forty miles and usually there were twenty-five to fifty head depending on the number of bulls. When rounding them up we tried to bunch twenty to fifty. The first day's loading was not too good, only sixteen or eighteen; but after that it went better. The train finally pulled out with two hundred head bound for Canada.

That day a crowd of Missoula hangers-on rode out to stop the loading, in protest against the buffalo going to Canada. Pablo convinced them he would be the only loser – so they finally rode off.

In the fall, Pablo had more trouble, he got sixty head into one corral, but the other two hundred were real rough. We chased them thirty-five miles, the horses were great. Well, we reached Ravalli and a locomotive went past. The buffalo broke and there was no thought of rounding them up that night.

Pablo talked to Charles Allard and agreed to pay him 2,000 dollars for forty-five to fifty extra cowboys under Allard, for five days. They finally cut the herd in two drives and sent them off; over two hundred head.

Howard and I did not see that, for when the buffalo scattered we took the train to see the Butte mines, time hung heavy at Ravalli. In Missoula it was customary for many to carry a shooting iron on the hip. One day, Ayotte,

Douglas and I were having a beer in the Missoula hotel situated on the corner of the Main Street. Suddenly two shots were fired in the street and the bat-wing doors flung open, and a man was sprawled, arms out, stretched at our feet. Howard and I took a high dive for the door to the hotel, next to our table. Where was Ayotte? On going back we found him sitting at the table with glazed eyes gazing into space, and his beer upset. Montana was still pretty rough.

I went down for the spring round-up but it was a lot of hard work and no results. Pablo had built a corral at a horseshoe bend on the Pend d'Oreille. He had built a very long fence over the river in a V-shape, into which the buffalo were driven. The point of the V ended at the corral and they went through this. We seemed to ride in bad luck and after getting about sixty together, they broke before we got them to the corral.

We finally managed to get about thirty rounded up but they were wild. Pablo had decided before this round-up to try crates on top of wagons to take the buffalo into Ravalli. He strung these wagons together, the crates open at each end except the last one. Four cowboys were on top of each crate to let down a gate effect as soon as a buffalo was in that crate. Sure the buffalo went in – even to the end of the train. Then things happened no one could describe. Talk about cyclone pictures of a town blown to pieces! In minutes, not a wagon was on four wheels, kindling wood and cowboys scrambling for ponies were all that one could see.

Pablo decided to get wagons ready for the next round-up but he swore that he would get them strong. He was sure a fine old fellow and his pride was hurt that he was not able to ship the animals he promised that year.

One day in 1909, we were loading. Pablo received a telegram. Loading stopped. Pablo caught the flyer to Missoula. The next day Pablo was on the job. It seems one of his sons killed a man. Nothing more was heard of the killing and the boy came back with Pablo. Then loading went on as usual.

I rode most of the time with the cowboys and came to know the country. One favourite break of the buffalo was to swim the Pend d'Oreille. I had taken a lot of photographs but wanted some swimming the river. So one day I stationed myself on the bank opposite where the buffalo would enter. After a long afternoon with cactus and rattlesnakes, buffalo started down the opposite bank. I got into a large tree in a position to take photographs. I took some dozen good pictures and noticed how high they swam, a man on the back would not get wet. All the buffalo had gone but one fine bull, standing up to his knees in water. I thought I would get down, keeping the trees between us, and get my horse. But nothing doing, every time I started he raised his tail. The devil kept me there over an hour until two punchers came along and how they did rag me. They roped him head and heels in a hurry and in a jiffy my model was turned into a steer.

I arranged with Pablo in 1909, to give him 100 dollars per head for any

"Sir Donald" in the Buffalo Park, Banff

buffalo accidentally killed. I collected a dozen bull heads and as many cows and robes. With the help of my horse I turned the carcass over after skinning one side. I used a belt hatchet to separate the head and neck. A load of one on a horse was enough for it to carry. I had to walk ten miles very often to get help to bring it in for treatment, and ship it to the buffalo train at Ravalli. I sure earned my buffalo.

There was always danger when the herd would charge back into the riders. Only once when a herd was stampeding over a very steep cut-bank did a Flathead Indian get between a buffalo and the river. He was on a small active pony but the horse was not quick enough to miss the bull, which caught it just at the Indian's foot, throwing them both into the sky above the buffalo's back. They crashed down the bank and the Indian was killed though the pony was all right.

The price of the buffalo had started at ninety dollars a head, but a feud developed between young Allard and Pablo. Allard was difficult to get along with and he was constantly keeping Pablo's cow pokes talked into doing half a job. We had to come to Pablo's rescue and the price went up. The Canadian government bought Allard off at so much per head delivered by him. Allard was not a good fellow.

Pablo had the reinforced box-topped wagons ready for 1909. One day we had seventy-five buffalo that we had driven into the natural corral using the wing fence. This was in the fall round-up. At the open end of the corral there was a snake fence of three foot timbers so we had an air tight enclosure. So we thought! We went to bed happy that night because we had been travelling in bad luck for the last three weeks. I awoke at daylight but I could not see across the corral nor could I hear the usual low grunt-talking of the buffalo. I climbed the nine foot fence to see and there was not a buffalo in sight. I alarmed the camp and we examined the fence while others followed around the edge of the cut-bank and found tracks of buffalo leading out onto the range. The buffalo, by working all night, had cut a switch-back path to the top from creek level. They had hooked and pawed a path up a bank a hundred feet high, moving yards and yards of earth and gravel. There was no doubt they were gone.

Pablo sure ran in bad luck, what with Allard and the buffalo break, I do not think he even got forty off that fall. He had done well enough in the spring, we seemed to load easier. It was a sight to see those wagons forty-five or fifty strung out and headed for Ravalli.

Charlie Russel came along in the fall and I guess the photographer with him had an experience something like mine, but at least I did not lose my camera. Russel sure could tell yarns and we all had good times at night around the fire. Joe Marion was a fine man and helped Pablo at every turn. I remember Joe Houle and George Sloan, we certainly had some good rides.

I decided to call it quits but in 1912 I guess Pablo had had enough of buffalo, he invited us down to hunt the last fifty or so buffalo left. The Montana government called it off so I never went back. Howard Douglas and I would have liked to see the boys and Pablo again, but we did not feel badly about the hunt. Old Howard was something like me, it was fine to kill to eat – but not much fun just for trophies.

In 1911, Banff got seventy-seven of the Pablo buffalo, seven of these were magnificent bulls. They still could not touch old "Sir Donald", which Sir Donald Smith had given to Banff. However, they replaced the old fellow who had been killed a couple of years before by a younger bull.

[It is of interest to note that this whole operation took considerably longer than was expected, and also the number of buffalo was much larger than first realized. The files at Elk Island Park reveal the following facts about the time and the number of buffalo received: June 1907-199, October 1907-211, none in 1908, July 1909-190, October 1909-28, June 1910-38, October 1910-28; May 1911-7, June 1912-7. So it took six years for Pablo to deliver 708 buffalo. In the 1911 shipment he sent 7 head of elk as well.– ed. note.]

BIBLIOGRAPHY

Alberta Historical Review, Summer 1957. *Quaker in Buckskin*, Gowan, E.P.
Archives of the Canadian Rockies, Banff, Alberta – Files:
    Anderson, J.R.– Bankhead
    Astley, C., Astley, W.
    Banff School – 20th Anniversary
    Board of Trade – Banff Advisory Council
    Craig, W.– Bankhead
    Fear, G., Fear, W.
    Fulmer, A.– People, Incidents, Organizations
    Green, H.U.– Trapping, Biology and Behaviour of the Wolverine, Ms.
    McAuley, C.H.– Bankhead
    McGuinness, Rev. R.– Catholic Church
    Movies
    Paris, C.– Early Skiing in Banff
    Sibbald, A.
    Simpson, J.– includes some Thorington copies
    Simpson, Mary and Margaret
    Unwin, E.E.– Sid Unwin, guide and Banff
    Warren, Mary Schaffer (Mrs. C.)
    Wilson, T.E.
    Woodworth, B., Woodworth, J.
Baillie-Grohman, W.A.– *Camps in the Canadian Rockies*
Baird, D.M.– *Banff National Park, How Nature Carved Its Splendour*
Banff Park – *The Globe*, Toronto, August, 15, 1885
Barbeau, M.– *Indian Days in the Canadian Rockies*
Barbeau, M.– *Indian Days on the Western Plains*
Begg, A.– *The Great Canadian North West*
Bell, M.– *Painters in a New Land*
Belyea, H.R.– *The Story of the Mountains in Banff National Park*
Bond, C.– *Surveyors of Canada 1867-1967*
Bradley, A.G.– *Canada in the 20th Century*
Brown, S. and Schaffer, Mrs. C.– *Alpine Flora of the Canadian Rockies*
Bundy, F.G.– *The Red Dragon of the Woods* – Forest and Outdoors, June 1929
Burpee, L.J.– *Among the Canadian Alps*
Burpee, L.J.– *LaVerendrye and His Sons*
Burpee, L.J.– *On the Old Athabasca Trail*
Burton, P.– *The Last Spike*
Byrne, A.R.– *Man and Landscape Changes in Banff National Park Before 1911*
Campbell, M.W.– *Lords of the North West*
Campbell, M.W.– *The North West Company*
Campbell, M.W.– *The Saskatchewan*
Camsell, C.– *Geology of Canadian National Parks*
Canadian Alpine Journals – Volumes: 1: 2(1): 2(2): 3: 4: 5: 6: 11: 12: 14: 18: 25(1): 27(2): 28(2): 29(1)
Canadian Geographic Journal – Barbeau, Marius, Feb. 1955
Canadian Historical Review – 1934, 1937, 1939
Canadian Medical Journal – July 14, 1962, Vol. 57 – "Sir James Hector"
Canadian Ski Annual 1932 – "Jasper to Lake Louise on Skis" – C. White
Carrel, F.– *Canada's West and Farther West*
Catlin, G.– *The North American Indians, 1841* Vol. 1 and Vol. 2
Chambers, E.J.– *The Unexploited West*
Chalmers, J.W.– *Fur Trade Governor,* George Simpson

Champlain Society – *Journal of Gabriel Franchere*
Champlain Society – *Narrative of David Thompson,* Edited by J.B. Tyrrell, 1916
Champlain Society – *The Papers of the Palliser Expedition*
Chapelhow, Iris – *Half a Century of Service*
Coker, R.E.– *Streams, Lakes, Ponds*
Coleman, A.P.– *Glaciers of the Rockies & Selkirks*
Coleman, A.P.– *The Canadian Rockies, Old and New Trails*
Coleman, A.P.– *The Last Million Years*
Coues, E.– *New Light on the Early History of the Greater North West*
    – Manuscript Journals of Alexander Henry and David Thompson
Cowan, I. McT. and Guiguet, C.J.– *Mammals of British Columbia*
Crag and Canyon – File at the Archives of the Canadian Rockies
DeSmet, Father P.J.– *Oregon Missions, Travels Over the Rocky Mountains 1845-46*
DeTremaudan, A.H.– *The Hudson Bay Road*
Dorst, J.– *Before Nature Dies*
Dugas, G.– *The Canadian West*
Edmonds, E.– "The Committees Punch Bowl" – The Beaver, Sept. 1948
Edwards, R.– *The Trail to the Charmed Land*
Elkington, E.W.– *Canada the Land of Hope*
Farb, P.– *Face of North America*
Fay, C.E.–"Casualty on Mount Lefroy" – Appalachia Vol. VIII 1896-98
Federal Government – Dept. of the Interior Reports:
    Chief Superintendents Reports 1911 –
    Commissioners Reports 1909 –
    Superintendents Reports 1887-1949
    Geological Surveys 1880-1930
    Topographical Surveys
    Triangulation Surveys
    Publications;
    Canada Calls You
    Canada's Mountain Playgrounds
Fleming, Sir Sandford – *From Old to New Westminster, A Summer Tour*
Fraser, E.– *The Canadian Rockies*
Freeman, N.R.– *On the Roof of the Rockies*
Gardner, J.– *Recent Glacial Activity and Some Associated Land Forms
    in the Rocky Mountains*
Geographic Board of Canada – *Place Names of Alberta*
Gibbon, J.M.– *Steel of Empire*
Grant, Rev. G.M.– "C.P.R. by the Kicking Horse Pass and the Selkirks,"
    The Week, Dec. 13, 1883
Grant, Rev. G.M.– *Ocean to Ocean Sandford Fleming's Expedition in 1872*
Grant, Rev. G.M.– *Picturesque Canada, Vol. 1*
Harman, D.W.– *Voyages and Travels*
Hedges, J.B.– *Building the Canadian West*
Henshaw, J.W.– *Mountain Wildflowers of Canada*
Holmgren, E.J. and Holmgren, P.M.– *Place Names of Alberta*
Holway, E.W.D.– "New Light on Mts. Hooker and Brown"
    – Canadian Alpine Journal, Vol. IX, 1918
Hopwood, V.G.– *David Thompson, Travels in Western North America*
Hornaday, W.T.– *Campfires in the Canadian Rockies*
Hosie, R.C.– *Native Trees of Canada*
Howay, F.W.– "David Thompson's Account of his First Attempt to Cross
    the Rockies", Queen's Quarterly, August 1933

Hudson's Bay Record Society:
   Hudson's Bay Company Vol. I – 1670-1788
   Simpson's Athabasca Journal – 1938
   Simpson's 1828 Journey to the Columbia
Hudson's Bay Company – Trade Dept.– *Canada's Fur Bearers*
Innis, H.A.– *The Fur Trade in Canada*
Innis, M.Q.– *Travellers West*
Irving, W.– *Astoria*
Kane, P.– *Wanderings of an Artist*
Kraus Reprint – *Life, Letters and Times of Father DeSmet,* Vol. 1
Lavender, D.– *The Fist in the Wilderness*
Lent, D.G.– *West of the Mountains, James Sinclair and the Hudson's Bay Company*
Longstaff, F.V.– Historical Notes on Glacier House
Luxton, N.K.– "When the Buffalo Came Back" – Unpublished Manuscript
MacGregor, C.– *Behold the Shining Mountains*
Mackenzie, A.– *Voyages to the Frozen Sea and the Pacific*
MacLeod, J.A.E.– "Old Bow Fort", Canadian Historical Review, Dec. 1931
Macoun, J.– Autobiography
Marsh, J.S.– *Man, Landscape and Recreation in Glacier National Park, B.C.*
   1880 to the Present, Thesis, University of Calgary, Calgary, Alberta.
McClintock, W.– *The Old North Trail*
McCowan, D.– *Hilltop Tales*
McCowan, D.– *Tidewater to Timberline*
McInnis, C.M.– *In the Shadow of the Rockies*
McInnis, E.– *Canada, A Political and Social History*
Milton and Cheadle – *A Trip Across Canada*
Mitchell, B.W.– *Trail Life in the Canadian Rockies*
Mitchner, E.A.– *William Pearce and Federal Government Activity in Western Canada*
   – Ph.D. Thesis, Dept. of History, University of Alberta
Moberly, H.J. and Cameron, W.B.– *When Fur Was King*
Moberly, W.– *Blazing the Trail Through the Rockies*
Moore, P.A.– *Lords of Lakes and Forests*
Morse, E.W.– *Fur Trade – Canoe Routes Then and Now*
Nelson, J.G. and Chambers, M.J.– Geomorphology
   – Process and Method in Canadian Geography
Patterson, R.M.– "We Climb the Pathless Pass", The Beaver, Autumn 1963
Pearce, W.– "Establishment of National Parks in the Rockies",
   Alberta Historical Review, Summer 1962
Phillips, W.J. and Niven, F.– *Colour in the Canadian Rockies*
Pierce, L.– *Our Dominion*
Potter, W.N.C.– *Traveller in a Vanished Landscape,*
   David Douglas Botanical Explorer
Putnam, W.L. and Boles, G.W.– *Climbers Guide to the Rocky Mountains*
Robert Rundle Papers – Publication of the Glenbow-Alberta Institute
   Nov.-Dec. 1971
Rundle, Rev. R.T.–"Original Diary", Glenbow-Alberta Institute Archives,
   Calgary, Alberta
Ryerson, Rev. J.– *Hudson's Bay Territory, 1855*
Scace, R.C.– *Banff – A Cultural History – Study of Land Use and Management*
   in the National Park
Schaffer, M.– *Old Indian Trails of the Canadian Rockies*
Schwartz, W.– *Voices for the Wilderness*
Scoyen, E.T.– *America's Living Heritage*
Shaw, C.A.– *Tales of a Pioneer Surveyor*

Simpson, Sir George – *Narrative of a Journey Around the World*
Slaymaker, O. and McPherson, H.J.– *Mountain Geomorphology*
Smith, J.K.– *David Thompson Fur Trader, Explorer, Geographer*
Smith, R.N.–"Settlement at Minnewanka" – Paper,
    Archives of the Canadian Rockies, Banff, Alberta
Southesk, Earl of – *Saskatchewan and the Rocky Mountains*
Spry, I.M.– "Routes Through the Rocky Mountains", The Beaver, Autumn, 1963
Stanley, G.F.G.– *Mapping the Frontier*
Stutfield, H.E.M. and Collie, J.N.– *Climbs and Exploration in the Canadian Rockies*
Taylor, W.C.– *The Snows of Yesteryear*, 1973
Thompson, D.W.– *Men and Meridians*, Vol. 2
Thorington, J.M.– "The Glittering Mountains of Canada", Alpine Journal, XXVII,
    No. 2, 1940
Tough, G.W.– *Study of Coal Mining in the Cascade Area*, M.A. Thesis,
    University of Calgary, Calgary, Alberta
Trail Riders of the Canadian Rockies, 1936-38
Turner Bone, P.– *When the Steel Went Through*
Tyrrell, J.B.– "Notes and Documents" – David Thompson and the
    Rocky Mountains, Canadian Historical Review, Vol. XV, 1934
Van Kirk, S.– *Development of National Park Policy in Canada's Mountain*
    National Parks, M.A. Thesis, University of Alberta, Edmonton, Alberta
Victor, E.A.– *Canada's Future*
Walhburn, S.– *Trails, Trappers and Tenderfeet in Western Canada*
Wallace, J.N.– *Passes of the Rocky Mountains*, M.A. Thesis, University of Alberta,
    Edmonton, Alberta
Warkentin, J.– *The Western Mountains of Canada*
Warre, Capt. H.– *Sketches in North America and the Oregon Territory*
Weiner, N. – *I Am a Mathematician*, 1956
Wheeler, A.O.– *The Selkirk Range*
Wilcox, W.D.– *Camping in the Canadian Rockies*
Williams, M.B.– *The Heart of the Rockies*
Williams, M.B.– *The Kicking Horse Trail*
Wilson, T.E.– File, Glenbow-Alberta Institute Archives, Calgary, Alberta
Wilson, T.E.– *Trail Blazer of the Canadian Rockies*

PHOTO CREDITS

Summerthought Publishing would like to thank the following individuals, museums, and archives for permission to reproduce their work.

Eleanor Luxton Historical Foundation: p. V
Glenbow Museum: front cover (NA-2977-37), p. 24 (NA-1241-388), p. 83 (NA-3026-37), p. 109 (NA-529-20),
Andrew Hempstead: p. VIII, p. 5, p. 16
Bob Smith: p. 13
Whyte Museum of the Canadian Rockies: p. 38 (NA66-2103), p. 44 (NA66-525), p. 55 (V527/P51-229), p. 58 (NA66-453), p. 67 (NA66-1629), p. 70 (NA-2977-1), p. 73 (NIA-0201), p. 78 (V48/NA65-226), p. 85 (NA66-1488), p. 87 (NA33-797), p. 89 (V178/PA240-12), p. 94 (Luxton collection), p. 98 (NA33-1885), p. 101 (NA66-1855), p 104 (V92/NG21), p. 107 (V484/NA29-334), p. 111 (Luxton collection), p. 113 (V469-1835), p. 119 (V263/NA71-3600), p. 120 (V263/NA71-3392), p. 122 (Luxton collection), p. 124 (Luxton collection), p. 125 (Luxton collection), p. 127 (PA139-347), p. 131 (V436/PA3-194A), p. 135 (V273/PD62-1), p. 139 (V692A-148), p. 141 (V263/NA71-3392), p. 143 (Luxton collection), p. 150 (Luxton collection)

INDEX